ENJOY YOUR GARDEN
GARDENING FOR EVERYONE

CHARLIE DIMMOCK

PENGUIN BOOKS

PENGUIN BOOKS

Published by the Penguin Group
Penguin Books Ltd, 27 Wrights Lane, London W8 5TZ, England
Penguin Putnam Inc., 375 Hudson Street, New York, New York 10014, USA
Penguin Books Australia Ltd, Ringwood, Victoria, Australia
Penguin Books Canada Ltd, 10 Alcorn Avenue, Toronto, Ontario, Canada M4V 3B2
Penguin Books India (P) Ltd, 11 Community Centre, Panchsheel Park,
New Delhi – 110 017, India
Penguin Books (NZ) Ltd, Cnr Rosedale and Airborne Roads,
Albany, Auckland, New Zealand
Penguin Books (South Africa) (Pty) Ltd, 5 Watkins Street, Denver Ext 4,
Johannesburg 2094, South Africa

Penguin Books Ltd, Registered Offices: Harmondsworth, Middlesex, England

First published by Michael Joseph 2000
Published in Penguin Books 2001
1

The photographic acknowledgements on page 233 constitute an extension of this copyright page

Set in Adobe Frutiger
Made and printed in Italy by Printer Trento Srl

I'd like to thank Jill and Tim, Tony, Grace and John, Ann-Marie and Tom for letting me invade their gardens to set up features for the book's photographs.

CONTENTS

INTRODUCTION

Most people are too busy working in the garden to relax and enjoy it. That's not my way. My approach may not come straight out of a gardening manual, but it's certainly much more fun.

There's a big difference between your own garden and one you just visit. With one that's open to the public, everything has to be done by the book – the garden has to stand up to heavy use because you get lots of feet over the lawns. It's got to be packed with complicated features and unusual plants because you want to attract visitors, who expect a cross between Kew Gardens and the Chelsea Flower Show. And you want things to last, because people want a garden to look like it's been there for ever.

At home it's completely different. You and your family and friends are the only people who'll use the garden, so it doesn't have to withstand an army of feet. You won't want to spend ages putting in features that make heaps of work, or – if you are anything like me – which are designed to last a lifetime. One of the good things about your own garden is being able to change things gradually or 'redecorate' when you feel like it. And unlike the professional gardener you don't have to spend ages learning loads of Latin names or perfecting back-breaking techniques. You can just do what you like.

I'm a professional gardener at work, but like most people I want to relax when I get home and that's how my rather laid-back style of gardening has come about. When anyone asks me about how to make a start, I just tell them go for it – forget about learning the ropes, make your dream garden now, and learn how to look after it as you go. Gardening really isn't as difficult as it's cracked up to be. Most of it is just common sense.

I started gardening when I could still hardly say the word. It runs in the family. My dad always had a fabulous garden, and my grandad worked as a gardener – so I just grew up with it. I went to two horticultural colleges, Sparsholt in Hampshire and Cannington in Somerset, and then to the Chelsea Physic Garden in London – which has one of the best collections of unusual herbaceous plants I know – to get some concentrated hands-on experience. They teach you to do everything properly. It is taken for granted that you are already a plant and garden fanatic or you wouldn't be there.

Mind you, that didn't stop me wanting to ship off round the world when I'd finished my training. I spent the next eighteen months back-packing round New Zealand, not doing anything very horticultural at all, unless you count a bit of fruit-picking. I've been keen on travel ever since. Holidays are what I work hard for – I'll buy a round-the-world air ticket and call in at places like Fiji and the Cook Islands en route to see family and friends in New Zealand, taking in a few gardens on the way (some of the best cared for you'll ever see are at Disneyland!).

But I'm back in harness now. My 'day job' is managing a water garden centre in Romsey, which I've done for eight years. Besides helping customers I also look after the display gardens, which run to about two acres, with a couple of others, and we also propagate and grow on most of the plants we sell there. So I get to keep my hands pretty dirty.

My own garden is tiny, and because I'm away from home such a lot filming, it's got to be really quick and easy to look after – the sort of place I want to go straight out to see when I get back from a trip, knowing I can slump into a sunlounger with a glass of wine, without having to worry about what needs doing. I really love sitting in the garden doing nothing except looking at the water – the River Test runs round three sides of my house – or watching bees buzzing round the flowers. I enjoy entertaining a few friends outdoors, lounging round the barbecue on a warm evening after work, and I get a big kick out of just wandering around doing odd jobs without any real urgency. I'll do odd bits of weeding in my bare feet – I love the feel of soil between my toes. Dead-heading is positively therapeutic if you have a glass of wine in one hand and just let relaxation waft over you.

That's the way lots of people would like to garden, if only they were 'allowed to', which is why I've pulled together here all my best tips and ideas for making the garden more fun. I promise not to overdose on Latin names, though I'm afraid there's no alternative sometimes, because not all plants have common names – and sometimes using the Latin one is the only way you can be sure of getting exactly the plant you want at a garden centre.

There are really just four rules for anyone taking a first stab at gardening my way.

Keep it simple. A simple garden can look stunning. The less you have, the less there is to look after, leaving you more time to enjoy it. And anyway, the 'less is more' look is very trendy.

Stick to easy plants – I reckon about 90 per cent of them are like that. Read the instructions on the labels and you won't go far wrong.

Get stuck in. Making a start is the hardest bit. With gardening, you learn a lot on the job. Once you know a few really basic things, like how to put a plant in properly, it's amazing how the pieces start to fall into place.

And the really important thing – have fun.

THE ESSENTIALS

You don't need to spend a fortune to start gardening. But there's only so much you can do with an old dinner fork; you really need a few bits of basic gardening gear. There's no need to go out and buy the top of the range, though. Start off with a budget collection that does the job, and spend the money you've saved on plants, some really good pots, or a pretty water feature instead. At least if you've got your own tools, there's a good chance the job will get done without waiting till you can borrow them!

Here's what I'd suggest you need to start off with:

*   **Spade.** For digging, and for making holes to put the bigger plants like shrubs and climbers in.
*   **Hand trowel.** For planting small plants, and some weeding.
*   **Hoe.** For quick weeding if you don't let the weeds get too big, when you have to do it by hand with a trowel.
*   **Rake.** For collecting up dead leaves and weeds, and straightening out gravel.
*   **Wheelbarrow** or **builder's bucket.** For carrying weeds away in, and for moving materials like compost, manure, gravel or bark chippings.
*   **Lawnmower** (if you've got a lawn). A small electric hover model without a grassbox is cheap, and quite enough for most small gardens if you don't let the grass grow too long.
*   **Hosepipe.** One and a half times the length of your garden so it reaches into all the difficult corners.

SCENTED THEMES

You know what it's like when you get off an aeroplane at a foreign airport at night? The first thing that hits you is that exotic scent that overpowers even the smell of aviation fuel – really strange and mysterious, but exciting too because it's the start of a holiday. A lot of scents remind me of places I've travelled. Tea tree oil takes me straight back to New Zealand. A friend's father has a 'batch' – a very basic holiday home – in the bush on Lake Taupo in North Island, surrounded by tea trees, and on a hot day the scent is intense. It's like wild aromatherapy. At home I've only got to put a few drops of the essential oil on the barbecue, and it's just like being back there again.

Frangipani reminds me of Fiji, but not for quite the same reasons. I once shared a tiny plane back from a remote island with a honeymoon couple whom the islanders had piled high with leis – floral necklets made of fresh frangipani flowers – for good luck. After an hour or so shut up in a confined space, the heat brought out the sickly scent of the flowers so strongly I thought I was going to pass out – I couldn't wait to get off the plane. Even now, I can't stand overpoweringly strong perfumes. So thanks all the same, but I'll just stick to a few easily recognizable floral whiffs wafting around the garden. I'm not one for a very girlie sort of garden, but I do like a few scented plants around the place. You can dot shrubs, climbers and flowers about and have a new selection of delicious scents coming on right round the year. Which is lovely – nice and natural, but not too much.

CONTAINERS

Scented plants are great for growing in containers. Because they are portable, they can be moved round the garden wherever and whenever you want. I like to stand scented containers next to doorways or under windows that are left open in summer, so the fragrance wafts into the house. They're good for creating a lingering atmosphere anywhere in the garden where you stop and sit. The patio is a natural choice for fragrant containers, but they don't have to be planted with flowers – herbs are wonderful too. And something scented is nice to put on the table when you're entertaining outdoors. Even a scented candle, stuck in a bowl of unscented plants, adds to the atmosphere.

Don't be taken in by what the catalogues say about scented plants. I often find the scent is nothing like they describe – nor anywhere like as strong. Sniff your way round and buy the ones that do something for you. I love lavender, but in small doses. Since it grows well in containers it's the sort of thing I'd use in a tub down the garden at one end of a seat, so I'm downwind of the odd waft. Another real favourite is basil, which is brilliant in pots on a patio. Its spicy savoury scent makes a pleasant change from over-sweet flowers in an area where you are going to be eating.

Much as I love basil, I've got to confess that I've never been very good at growing it. A friend gave me some very good tips. He has a restaurant down the road in Romsey, where he grows loads of basil in big tubs just outside the door for decoration, and lots more down the garden which they hack at for cooking. 'You over-water it, Charlie,' he said. 'You've got to wait till it's almost falling over, then give it a good soaking and leave it alone till next time.' He also tells me you shouldn't water basil before midday. What's so annoying is that he seems to be right. Just wait till I start giving him cookery tips!

There are two kinds of scented plants, the ones with perfumed flowers and those with aromatic leaves. Plants with strong-scented flowers, like lavender, are the sort that waft their scent around so you don't have to get your nose right on top of them. This makes them OK at a distance. Weaker-scented flowers like petunias are best in hanging baskets, window-boxes and on balconies, as scent tends to be concentrated when the air is warm and still – somewhere very sheltered like a patio is the perfect place for them. Plants with aromatic leaves, like herbs, need growing where you can run your fingers through the foliage. You've got to bruise these plants gently to release the oils that carry the scent, so grow them by a seat or at the side of a path where you can brush against them easily. Plants with scented leaves have one big advantage over scented flowers, though. They keep their perfume all the time, not just when the flowers are open.

One big container is much easier to look after than lots of little ones, so instead of the small 'multiple' herb pots you often see I've chosen a strawberry planter which looks the same but bigger. As it holds lots more soil the herbs won't need watering so often. Since a big container like this will be heavy when it's full of compost and plants, stand it in its final position while you plant it so you don't have to move it again.

1. **Put a handful of bits of broken clay flower pot in the bottom of the container. These stop your potting compost running out through the big drainage hole in the bottom, but allow surplus water to drain away quickly.**

2. **Using John Innes potting compost, a soil-based compost which is good for plants that stay in the same container long-term, fill the pot up to the first row of planting holes.**

3. **Tip the first plant out of its pot and, keeping its ball of roots intact, push it gently into one of the planting holes. Firm the compost gently round the root-ball, so that the hole is well stoppered.**

4. **Plant a different herb into each of the bottom row of holes, then tip in some more potting compost – enough to reach the next row of holes – and plant herbs in each of these too.**

5. **Fill the pot with compost almost to the rim, and then plant the biggest, most colourful herb, like the lavender I've used, in the top. Make sure you tuck the last of the compost round its roots – they all need to be covered. Then water the container well, using a slow trickle of water or a watering can with a rose to avoid washing the compost away.**

2

4

SCENTED PLANTS FOR CONTAINERS

Summer garden shows, even little local ones, are good places to find scented plants, as all the unusual plant nurseries sell them there. Any of the following are good compact kinds, ideal for containers.

Scented-leaved pelargoniums. These are my favourite scented plants, but if you are expecting 'geraniums' with big bright flowers *and* perfumed foliage, forget it. The two are related but they look completely different. Scented-leaved pelargoniums have subtle flowers and attractively textured foliage which can be all sorts of odd shapes: some are like oak leaves, others narrow and frilly, making patterns like old lace. There are loads of different varieties, each with a different smell – rose, lemon, cinnamon, orange, clove and pine. They are not hardy, so they need winter protection – keep them in a light, frost-free place such as your porch or under the carport if you don't have a sunroom, to save them for next year.

Lavenders ▶ Some varieties grow huge and straggly, so choose compact varieties for containers as they stay neat and bushy. The best-scented are 'Hidcote' and 'Munstead', French lavender (*Lavandula stoechas*), which has scented foliage as well as flowers, and woolly lavender, which has silver-felted foliage. These all have purple flowers. Bees love lavender, so keep the plants away from the table when you are eating or drinking to avoid sudden panics in susceptible friends.

Herbs. Any of the more compact herbs are good, but I specially like purple sage, which looks like it sounds, and also tricolour sage which has pink, cream and green variegated leaves – you can use them both for cooking as well as decoratively. Mint is good. I like the eau-de-cologne sort, which smells gorgeous and doesn't grow too big – it's great in containers, and wards off flies. The variegated mints are good too, but they don't have all that much scent – there's ginger mint, which has gold speckles, and the green and white pineapple mint. The good thing about growing mints in containers is that it makes them very easy to water. Because they like wet soil, you can just grow them in pots without drainage holes and top them right up every few days without worrying about overwatering.

CARING FOR PLANTS IN CONTAINERS

Containers need regular attention. If you don't have much time, restrict yourself to no more than about three tubs, especially if you plant them with bedding plants which need lots of water. If you do nothing else with containers, do the watering. A few weeks after planting, they'll be full of roots and will need watering at least once a day, more in hot or windy weather. Scented plants like lavenders and perennial herbs are less effort,

as they actually smell stronger if they are kept slightly on the dry side – but even they need watering every few days to stop them going brown or dying. Once a week, add a few drops of liquid feed to the water. If you think you are going to forget, mix a handful of slow-release fertilizer granules into the potting compost instead, before you plant the container – this will last all season. The only other thing to remember, to keep containers flowering all summer, is to nip off the dead flower-heads when they are over. You can use scissors, but I find it very relaxing to nip them off with my fingers while I'm wandering round enjoying the garden after work. Take a glass of wine with you – it makes all the difference.

OTHER IDEAS

CHEAT'S SCENT

It doesn't matter if you don't have the right plants to make a scented container, because you can always cheat. I do it all the time. I once had some lovely big begonias in a tub. You know, those really vulgar frilly ones that don't have any scent? And because I was expecting some friends for a meal I thought I'd jazz them up a bit, so I sprayed the flowers with some essential rose oil diluted with a bit of water. The first thing my friends did was plunge their noses into these great big frilly flowers – I mean, they *do* look as if they ought to be scented – and they were completely fooled. A few bottles of different flower oils are very useful for all sorts of special little touches in the garden. You can buy them all over the place nowadays – in chemists, health food shops and often even in the sort of garden centres that do gifts. Sink an empty flower oil bottle into a container of plants after using the oil in the bath, and it gives the plants just a faint 'aura'. Or tie up small bundles of joss-sticks with raffia, and push them in among plants in a container. You don't even need to light the sticks, as the scent will just 'leak out' gently over several weeks.

Another thing you can do is add scented plants to non-perfumed varieties to pep them up a bit. Night-scented stocks are good for this. They are well-known for their scent but are nothing special to look at, so I'll often sprinkle a few seeds into the compost round prettier but fragrance-free plants in a container. They grow very quickly and easily so you don't need to mess about with them. Just let them grow where the seeds fall. They flower about 10 weeks later.

TOP TIP

SCENTED TABLE CENTRE

If you just want a quick scented table centre for a dinner party or barbecue, you don't have to plant up a long-lasting container. Get a pretty bowl and stand three or four pots of compact aromatic plants, like scented-leaved pelargoniums or basil, in it. Fill the gaps between the pots with bark chippings, small fir-cones, or pebbles. Sprinkle a few more

over the compost to hide the pots. You can leave an arrangement like this until the plants get too big, or get past their best, and then just lift out the odd one and replace it, or take them all out and start again.

HERB SEATS

Gardening isn't just about having lots of colourful flowers – you can make some very good schemes using mainly foliage. That's one reason why I'm so keen on herbs: there are so many shades of green, as well as all the gold, silvery and variegated kinds, and lots of textures from smooth and shiny to rough and furry. The scent of herbs is incredibly relaxing, which is what makes them so good for a seat. They naturally grow best in the same sort of sunny sheltered spots we like to relax in. When you sit on creeping herbs, your weight crushes the leaves just enough to release the fragrance without harming the plants, and you can just drift off in a haze of perfume. Working weekends at the garden centre in summer, I sometimes get the odd afternoon off during the week instead, and this is just the way I like to spend that precious time – it's wonderful when you are feeling really tired. And since herbs have something for all the senses, including touch, a seat makes it possible to enjoy the lot at once.

People think herb seats are purely decorative, and they do look good, but they really are OK to sit on, too. You can make big bench seats, but I like the idea of a personal single-seater which is very quick and easy to make. Just use an ordinary wooden plant container like a half-barrel, a tub or a square planter, with some plain wooden trellis or an old chair-back from a junk shop nailed up the back. This won't be strong enough to lean back on, unless it's up against a wall, but you can fill the container with compost and plant it with creeping herbs, then train an upright variety of lavender or rosemary up the back. Personally, though, I'm still a bit off rosemary, as I had a definite overdose of it in New Zealand. For ten weeks before Christmas the vineyard I lived and worked at laid on big corporate parties for 100 to 150 people at a time. Since they made their own wine, and their neighbours ranched sheep, the deal was all the wine you could drink with salads and spit-roast lamb cooked with rosemary – they'd barbecue four at a time over vine prunings – and you could just keep helping yourself. Guess who got given the leftovers? The live-in workers. By Christmas we were really fed up with it, and you could even see the dogs go 'Oh no, not rosemary and lamb again' and just turn their noses up and walk off.

MAKING A TUB SEAT

An ordinary garden tub makes a good base for a herbal seat. I prefer to use a square wooden one – a round ceramic pot tends to look too much like an outdoor loo when it's used in this way. Herbs need a sheltered sunny spot to do well, so they like exactly the same sort of places we enjoy sitting and relaxing in – the patio is perfect, or a suntrap down the garden. But let the herbs cover the seat thickly before you start sitting on them too much, or they'll get worn out.

1. **Nail a bit of trellis to your tub to make the chair-back. Put some bits of broken clay flower-pot in the bottom for drainage, since herbs don't like boggy soil, then fill the tub with a gritty potting compost. You'll need to make your own, by mixing 4 parts of John Innes compost to 1 part of coarse sand (ask for potting sand at a garden centre).**

2. **Level the compost roughly and make 2 planting holes at the back of the 'seat'. You could use a small trowel if you like to stay neat and tidy but I just use my hands.**

3. I'm putting 2 rosemary plants along the back of the seat – I deliberately chose ones that had grown rather two-dimensional to give it a nice flat back. Bushier plants would take up the whole seat and spoil the shape, but if you can only find bushy plants, just cut out complete stems from the front and back of each plant to make them flatter. To keep the shape as they grow, tie the stems to the trellis and cut back any sticking-out shoots occasionally.

4. Fill the 'seat' with camomile plants – this is Roman camomile, which stays short but has neat double flowers, unlike the proper lawn camomile which doesn't have any flowers at all. Plant them about 4 inches apart so they cover the seat quickly and make a deep bouncy cushion.

3

MAKING A TUB SEAT

Herb farms have the biggest range of varieties and many sell by mail order. Don't just go for the usual 'cooking' varieties. You can often find variegated kinds which look more striking and are also well-scented. The best herbs to grow in a seat are the kinds that are naturally as short and flat as possible, so go either for truly creeping varieties that lie flat along the ground, or the short bushy spreading types that make natural low cushion shapes. Don't use plants that snap easily, like lavenders and sages, as they don't like being sat on. Camomile and thymes are the best for seats. Rosemary is good too, if you use one of the prostrate or bushy kinds.

My favourites are:

Creeping thymes. The gold-speckled 'Doone Valley' is good for foliage colour; choose the really low creeping varieties of wild thyme such as 'Annie Hall' if you want lots of flowers; caraway thyme (*Thymus herba-barona*) and 'Lemon Curd'

have specially delicious sharp, fresh, herby scents.

Camomile ◄ The non-flowering 'Treneague' form is the one sold for making camomile lawns, so it's brilliant for seats. Or use Roman camomile, which has loads of double daisy-like flowers. Both have delicious apple-scented foliage. Other kinds of camomile grow too tall for seats.

Rosemary. Prostrate rosemary or bush varieties like 'Severn Sea' are best for seats. *Rosmarinus lavandulaceus* has a lovely balsam scent but isn't very winter-hardy. Choose upright varieties like 'Miss Jessopp's' or the variegated 'Silver Spires' for seat backs.

CLIPPING HERBS

Upright herbs such as lavender and some kinds of rosemary make good miniature 'hedges' that are perfect for edging herb features or flower-beds as well as for herbal seat-backs, or you can use dwarf box for a more formal edging – this is often used in those geometric-shaped herb gardens. But they all need clipping to keep them in shape. Clip lavender or rosemary once a year, shortly after flowering. Dwarf box needs doing

in late spring and late summer to keep it looking neat (but don't use this for making chair-backs, as it smells of tomcat). Clip a herb lawn with shears in midsummer if it really needs it – don't do it later or it'll look scruffy in winter. Use scissors or sheep-shears, which you use one-handed, to clip herbs, or for large areas use normal hedging shears – not electric hedge-trimmers, as they are too big. I do the job by eye – if it's slightly uneven don't worry about it, as the natural look is 'in'.

OTHER IDEAS

* If you want a really solid type of herb seat that will be a permanent feature of the garden, you could make a bench-style seat out of brick, but this will need more serious construction.
* A very simple herb bench can be made using a wooden chest, with the lid up to form the back. There are often Shaker-style ones for sale in the garden-gadget brochures that drop out of the Sunday supplements, for storing boots or gardening tools. Or you could buy an old pine chest from a junk shop and paint it with coloured wood preservative or treat it to a stencil job. To stop the damp potting compost rotting the wood, line it with thick polythene first.
* If you go for the antique look, you can get one of those reproduction Edwardian wire garden seats and sit it over a container of herbs so the tops just reach up through the mesh of the seat, like a herbal cushion. Then you can change the scent of the seat any time you like just by switching the container of herbs.
* Instead of growing upright herbs over the seat-back, you could use evergreen euonymus for an all-year-round effect, or annual climbing flowers like sweet peas (good for scent). But if you choose flowering plants you'll have to keep the seat for decorative use only, as the flowers will get crushed.

AROMATIC LAWNS AND PERFUMED PATHS

Walking barefoot in the garden is what makes summer worth waiting for. I love the feel of the soft springy textures of plants underfoot, so a herb lawn is my idea of heaven. You can really go strong on scents. Unlike a patio, where concentrated plant perfumes can be overpowering, when you walk over a carpet of herbs you just get waves of herbal fragrances wafting up all round you – wonderful.

A herb lawn is great fun – a really sensuous, fragrant 'special occasion' feature that positively invites you to wiggle your toes in it. And it's lovely to lie on, on a warm summer evening after dinner, while you watch the stars – like a big squashy scented mattress. A circular herb lawn looks great in a modern garden, surrounded by a ring of cobbles, or in a formal garden you could put a brick path round it. You could make a herb lawn around an irregular area of paving in a contemporary garden, so the two sort of meld together. It's ideal for a small secluded area, with maybe a seat, where you don't have to walk on it regularly. But don't get the idea you can just use a carpet of herbs instead of your normal lawn. It isn't for everyday use – you don't want children or dogs romping on it – as it gets tatty very quickly. You also need the right sort of garden, with very well-drained soil and in a place that gets sun all day. But in the right spot . . . magic.

A more practical alternative for most of us is a herb path. It's just like a herb lawn but on a smaller scale so it's easier to fit into a small garden. And if it's in a place you need to walk on a lot, just sink 'stepping stones' in it so you can walk on those.

MAKING A HERB PATH

If you don't have room for a whole herb lawn, you can use the same technique to make a herb path. Well-drained soil is essential, otherwise your herbs will die in the first wet winter, so dig lots of grit into the ground – about 2 bucketfuls per square metre – then level the soil and spread 2 inches of gravel over the top before you start planting.

1. **Stand your plants about 6 inches apart so you can see where they are all going to go. If you want to economize and you don't mind waiting a bit longer before they cover the ground, you could increase the spacing to 12 inches apart. To plant, move each pot aside and scoop out a pot-sized hole.**

2. Lift the soil out – don't worry if some goes on the gravel, it'll clean up naturally next time it rains. Put the spare soil into a bucket as you go. Tip the plant out of its pot and fit the rootball into the hole, leaving the top inch sticking out of the ground. Firm the soil back round it, then sweep the gravel back so the plant ends up flush with the surface. Dead easy.

MAKING A HERB PATH

LOW SPREADING KINDS ARE ESSENTIAL

Camomile. For a romantic camomile lawn, you need the non-flowering form of camomile called 'Treneague', but I'd mix it with some Roman camomile which is equally compact but has lots of little double daisy flowers too. They are also nice dried and put in pot-pourri indoors.

Thyme ▶ You don't often see thyme lawns, but they are really delightful. You can use all the same variety if you want – I'd choose the wild thyme, *Thymus serpyllum* – or plant irregular patches of different varieties of creeping thyme to make a patchwork quilt effect, which looks brilliant. But watch out for bees if you like to walk barefoot over it.

OTHER IDEAS

HERB PATH ALTERNATIVES

* If you happen to be making a new gravel path, you can make it into a scented path by following the recipe for a herb lawn, but in a narrow path shape.
* If you have an existing hard path, you can plant spreading herbs along each side of it – low creeping kinds like camomiles and thymes will creep out over the path so you tread on them, or you could grow a low hedge of lavender along each side which you'll brush past so that you still get the atmosphere.
* If you have existing paving you can tuck a few herbs into wide gaps between paving slabs, so long as there is soil underneath and not mortar. Dig out some of the old soil to make a planting hole, mix a little potting compost in with the soil that is already there, and plant. Sprinkle a layer of fine grit round the plants afterwards.

OTHER IDEAS

SCENTED ADVENTURE TRAIL

Another good way to introduce lots of scent to a garden is by making a scented trail. This is just a route round the garden with scented plants dotted along the way. Plan it out a bit like a maze, so you find something new round every corner, and with a few blind alleys to pause in. Make sure there's enough room between the scented plants so you have lost the scent of one before you start getting whiffs of the next, or you lose what's special about it and just end up with one big face-full of scents you can't tell apart.

You could build on this idea and turn it into a complete adventure trail by adding a few rustling grasses and soft furry 'touchy-feely' plants, and I'd want a splashy fountain for running water effects, or a wind-chime hanging from a tree which sounds much the same. At the garden centre we have wide wooden ones which make a really restful low hollow booming sound. This way you would be giving your senses a real work-out, and

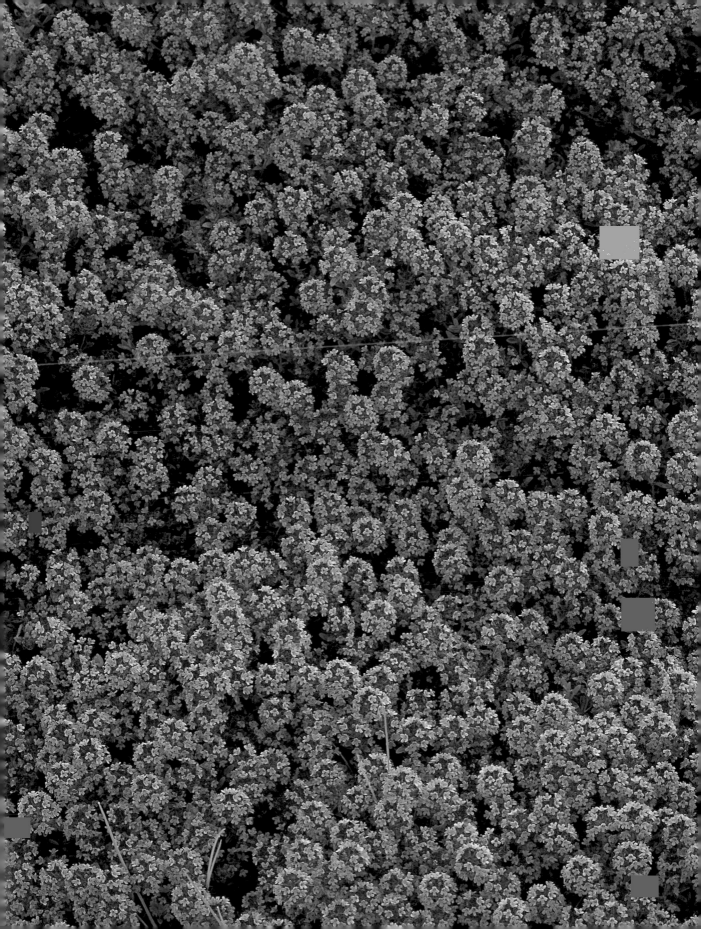

it's the sort of thing you can do even in a small garden. Children love it, but it's pretty good if you just happen to like wandering round the garden after work with a glass of wine.

Scented flowers. Chocolate cosmos is essential for chocoholics; pinks, hyacinths and lily-of-the-valley are well-known for their strong scents in spring, and lavender is a firm summer favourite.

Scented shrubs. My top three would be philadelphus (mock orange), *Viburnum carlesii* and lilac, which all have clear flowery fragrances.

Scented climbers and wall shrubs. The flowers of the pineapple broom (*Cytisus battandieri*) really smell of pineapple and look a bit like small pineapples too, while climbing roses and honeysuckle are old country garden classics.

Shrubs for winter fragrance. *Lonicera fragrantissima*, *Mahonia japonica* and *Eleagnus ebbingei* are all subtle rather than strong, so you only appreciate them when they are planted close to a path.

Soft furry plants. *Salvia argentea* has big soft silvery leaves like silky dinner plates, and *Stachys lanata* has shaggy silver leaves like rabbits' ears.

Sounds. Miscanthus grasses rustle in the breeze, and quaking grass has seedheads that tremble in the slightest breath of wind, making the tiniest whispering noise.

TOP TIP

TAKING CUTTINGS OF HERBS

If you need a lot of herbs, it works out quite expensive if you have to buy them. But you can always grow your own instead. Take cuttings of thyme, sage, rosemary and lavender in midsummer. Just snip 2 to 3 inches from the tips of the shoots, strip off the bottom leaves, and push the cuttings into pots of seed compost. Water, then slip a large plastic bag over the top of each pot. Keep them on a shady windowsill, and water only if they get dry. They will root in about 2 to 3 months. Pot each one individually and keep them in a safe place, where they will be regularly watered, until they are as big as the herb plants you buy in a garden centre. Then they are ready for planting. Starting with half a dozen 'stock plants', you could grow enough herbs for a small herb lawn in a year or eighteen months, but taking cuttings is a good way to get new plants to replace old worn-out ones anywhere in the garden. Especially the ones you cut hard for cooking.

SCENTED WATER FEATURE

Perfume and water are perfect partners, and some of my favourite garden features team the two together. Though few genuine water plants have any fragrance to speak of, there are lots of ways you can combine water with scented dry-land plants. Humid air 'magnifies' scent, so if you want to intensify the fragrance of flowers, then growing them close to a pond or fountain is a good way to do it. At the garden centre there's a huge honeysuckle by the river and I often catch lovely wafts of scent drifting across to my garden on the breeze on summer evenings. If you don't happen to have a river handy, you can get a similar effect on a smaller scale using a container of water with scented plants nearby – or just add a few drops of aromatherapy oil. One of my favourite unwritten rules of gardening says: 'When all else fails, cheat!'

You don't need a proper pond to enjoy a stunning water feature in the garden. A small bowl makes a good 'pond' to put on a table. If you have a really beautiful bowl, it looks good just on its own with water in it. My current favourite right now is a beautiful Chinese glazed bowl – it's not just any old bowl, but the sort people once used for showing exhibition goldfish in, you know, your prize-winning black moor, the one with the goggly eyes. Mine is decorated inside and out with painted plant and flower designs. It would be lovely on the patio with a few drops of rose oil in it, surrounded by pots of plants. Or you could make a miniature floating garden. For this you need a bowl half full of water and on top you place just a single floating water plant. Use water lettuce or water hyacinth, which have lovely sculptural shapes. This works well in a big china salad bowl, but it also looks lovely in a clear glass bowl, where you can see all the trailing roots as well.

If you want something bigger, you can make a very attractive water garden in a container, which makes an unusual yet easily maintained centrepiece for a patio, and then just grow scented climbers all round. The warmth and the walls of the patio bounce the scent back at you, so you can just sit back and enjoy it. The combination of warmth on your skin, scent in the air and water to watch is really therapeutic – you can feel the stress melting away. Just use a huge pot – the sort meant for growing plants in, but without any drainage holes in the bottom. All you do is fill the container with water and stand it on the paving, with a water-lily or water hawthorn inside – they are sold growing in planting baskets all ready to be stood in place.

Instead of plants and fish, you might like to have a fountain in your container of water. It's just as easy to do, and looks incredibly effective. Take a wide bowl or ceramic planter without drainage holes and at least 6 inches deep. Fill it with water and put the smallest solar-powered fountain you can get in it – the floating type is fine for this. It'll be enough to give you a decent spray, but it's not so big all the water goes over the edge of the bowl and empties it. When the sun isn't shining, the spray will be a bit smaller – but that won't matter. It only takes about 3 minutes to put it all together, and you don't need the bother of laying on electricity. It's a real doddle. One last tip – this is the perfect place to use the aromatherapy oil trick. Just put a few drops in the water. The oil gets swirled round by the fountain and sprayed up into the air with the water, which makes the scent seem more lingering.

POND IN A POT

This is the very cheapest and easiest kind of water feature, but one of the most versatile.

1. Choose a large ceramic bowl; this one was originally a fruit bowl so it holds water anyway, but if you use a plant container you'll need to bung up the drainage holes in the bottom. Use corks or round stones, seal them with clear silicon (which they sell in water garden centres for sealing aquariums), and leave for a few days to dry. Put a few clean, smooth stones in the bottom, then fill the bowl with tap water. Leave for a few days to disperse the chlorine.

2. Float a handful of fairy moss (azolla) on top, add a few drops of aromatherapy oil for the scent, and that's all there is to it. Simple but stunning.

3. You can use the same basic idea to make an outdoor 'goldfish garden'. Remember, though, not to use the aromatherapy oil!

2

3

THE BASICS CARING FOR A POTTED POND

Unlike more complicated ponds this sort is almost maintenance-free.

In summer just top up the water level weekly, as you can lose an inch of water a week by evaporation in a hot or breezy spot. In winter you need to protect a mini-pond from freezing, as this will crack the container as well as killing the plants and any fish. Move the container into a sunroom or enclosed porch or carport where it can't freeze solid, or, for larger containers, put an electric pond heater inside. But if you can't do either of those, just take out the plants and store the container upside down to stop it filling with rainwater. Catch the fish first and keep them in a tank indoors until spring. You'll need to replace the plants anyway when you set up next year's water feature – so if this is your only winter storage option I'd use water hyacinth or water lettuce which die off in winter anyway.

SCENTED PLANTS

Water-lilies. It really annoys me the way water plant catalogues crack on about scented water-lilies. Yes, there are some – look for *Nymphaea odorata* varieties if you want to sniff for yourself – but they would need a very big container to grow happily in a container water feature. Still, if you had a tank of water on the patio, 1 to 2 feet deep and 2 to 3 feet across, it would certainly be worth going for one of these. A nicely enclosed patio is about the only place you are really going to notice the perfume of a 'scented' water-lily – in a pond, it just gets lost on the breeze.

Water hawthorn ▶ The only water plant I can really call perfumed is water hawthorn, which has a lovely musky scent that is most noticeable in the evening. At work, one of my jobs is propagating water plants, which we do in a glasshouse. When it's full of water hawthorn, customers always comment on the tremendous fragrance that gets trapped inside. But because I'm in there every day, I'm so used to it, I don't even notice it any more. Water hawthorn is a brilliant plant, with floating leaves and strange white flowers rather like melted candle stubs floating amongst them, but what's specially good about it is the way it stays small enough to grow in a reasonable-sized container, say 2 feet across and 9 inches or more deep.

Jasmine is brilliant, a very exotic hint-of-the-Orient type of perfume that goes well with heat, and it flowers most of the summer. *Jasminum officinale*, the common white jasmine, is the most reliable – don't get winter jasmine by mistake, because besides only flowering in winter, it doesn't have any scent.

Trachelospermum jasminoides also has a jasmine scent, but with big creamy-white whiskery-centred flowers; it's a bit more exotic looking than white jasmine and has oval evergreen leaves. If you really like tropical-strength perfume, you could plant both together – they flower at the same time, all through the summer, and the scents 'go together'.

Clematis aren't usually scented, but there are a few species with a faint subtle scent which is great on the patio. They don't have the huge wide open flowers of the big hybrid clematis, but they are lovely anyway. Look for *Clematis armandii*, which is evergreen and has white flowers in spring, *Clematis montana* 'Elizabeth', which has single pink flowers in early summer, the same shape as a normal clematis but only about an inch across, or *Clematis rehderiana*, which has small tubular yellow flowers in late summer and autumn which smell like cowslips.

SCENTED PLANTS FOR AN EXISTING POND

If you have a bigger natural-style pond down the garden, grow one or two scented marginal plants in baskets standing on the shallow shelf round the edges. There aren't all that many – the best known is water mint. This has scented leaves – but like most mints, it tends to take over unless you divide it up every year or two. Then there's the orange-peel plant, pictured below. You know when you eat oranges with some of the

pith on? It smells just like that tastes. Talk about good marketing – the Latin name, *Houttuynia cordata*, is unspeakable. It's a nice-looking plant, with green heart-shaped leaves and white flowers, but like most plants with scented leaves you only get the scent if you actually bruise the leaves. Most people grow the variegated version of it, 'Chameleon', which has prettier leaves but no scent to speak of. There is one more scented water plant, but it's a bit unusual so you may have trouble finding it. We grow it at the garden centre, and it's called water spearmint (*Preslia cervina*). It's rather like a mint, but it's got a really intense sweet spearmint smell which you either like or you don't. I've been working with it for ten years, and after a day spent potting it up, your hands smell like pure chewing-gum. I'm still not sure if that's what I want round the garden.

MEDITERRANEAN SCHEMES

My dad has a place in Portugal which is great for a family holiday. It's really relaxing there – perfect for just pottering around. Next door there lives an old couple – he's ninety-three and she's eighty-nine, but they are both incredibly fit and still farming. (It must be down to the Mediterranean diet, and all that fresh air.) When I'm there they often drop round to see us. It's quite a shock when you are sunbathing – talk about quick cover-up. They always ask us round for a drink. Their tipple is neat scotch, in lethal shots. You can't refuse but, being a girl, I only get one, thank goodness. On their land they've got olive groves, pomegranates and some carob trees. They make good money for carob beans but they don't actually grow them – the trees just happen to be there, so they harvest them.

The little paths between the fields round the house are full of wild flowers, and it's great fun spotting what grows naturally. A favourite of mine which grows wild all over the place is the perennial morning glory. One day we drove past a big patch of it, and Dad said he'd always wanted some to grow in the garden. We stopped, but all the seedpods had already popped, and he still hasn't got any. It's no good trying a garden centre. The Portuguese ones are hopeless. With so many garden-mad English people over there, you'd think they would sell things like olive trees which everyone wants, but all they stock is fussy little flowers. Maybe one day I'll start my own nursery out there. . .

DROUGHT GARDEN

Water is always a problem in the Mediterranean region – no wonder it's the original home of the drought garden. It's amazing what they can achieve with very little water. You see wonderful courtyards tucked away behind impressive wrought-iron gates, overflowing with sculptured fruit trees like citrus, pistachio and figs mixed with evergreen shrubs, fountains and paving – but never lawns, as they'd be too much trouble in that climate. Now that hot dry summers and water meters are becoming a regular feature in the UK, we are seeing lots more water-saving gardens here, too. Ingredients like gravel, pebbles, spiky shrubs and drought-proof perennials and grasses make a glamorous garden that's practical, quick and easy to care for, so you can spend your time soaking up the sun instead of worrying about watering.

My ideal Mediterranean-style garden would be very simple, but stunning and easy to do – and no trouble to look after. I'd just go for a tree for shade, with a few perennials and grasses, and some architectural features like a seat and some paving and a few plants in pots. In an ideal world I'd plan the garden around an existing old gnarled tree – a cork oak would be my first choice in a real Mediterranean setting. If there wasn't one, what I'd do is cheat, and plant something new but with bags of character.

A fig tree would be perfect. Figs say 'Mediterranean' loud and clear. They have great big leaves and naturally grow into the most amazing shapes if you just plant them in the open and leave them alone. People pay a fortune for that kind of 'distressed' look. If your tree looks too well behaved, you can help it along by nipping out the odd shoot here and there to encourage it to grow more gnarled. You can prune a fig tree very hard – only in midwinter, or else it bleeds – to keep it compact enough for even a small garden, but if you don't have enough room for a free-standing tree, you can plant a fan-trained fig that grows flat against a sunny wall, without losing its knotty character.

Or you can grow a fig in a pot – this keeps it naturally compact, and it has the advantage of being portable so you can rearrange the garden whenever you feel like it. Because it is quite drought-tolerant, a fig is a good tree for a pot as it won't mind if you forget the occasional watering. To go with the tree, I'd put a few drought-proof perennials with lots of large flattish pebbles between them – they look specially great with grasses. Besides making a stunning contrast with the flowers, pebbles act as a stone mulch, helping to hold water in the soil.

A larger garden will take a lot more filling, but rather than cramming it with plants I would just go for a bigger version of the same sort of thing. I'd have a paved patio with a few citrus plants or oleanders in large tubs, and instead of a single tree I'd have several 'character' trees that really stand out among paving, gravel or pebbles, with occasional groups of well-chosen Med-style shrubs. A bit of statuary and a bench with maybe a couple of big empty pots tipped over on their side in a carpet of drought-proof plants, and there's your garden. And there's nothing to do but enjoy it.

WHAT TO GROW FOR MEDITERRANEAN CHARACTER

Not all plants that create a Mediterranean-looking garden actually come from the Mediterranean, though they usually come from places with hot dry summers so they make good easy-going drought-proof plants that suit this style of garden.

CHARACTER TREES

Italian cypress (*Cupressus sempervirens*). This is one of the classic trees that appears throughout the Med region, the tall thin pointy one. People always think it won't grow anywhere else, but it does fine here. One on its own looks like an exclamation mark, so I'd grow it with some of the more glamorous shrubs. At college, we were always getting into trouble for tying the top of the Italian cypress down to the ground, so the tree made a big arch – when it was untied, it stayed put and it was a real problem to get it straight again. Still, that's students for you.

Pride of India (*Koelreuteria paniculata*). This makes a stunning specimen tree to grow all on its own, a real gem. It makes me think of exotic holidays (so what else is new!). This is a brilliant small tree with a great shape all year, and stunning foliage that is red-tinged when it first unrolls in spring, and turns bright gold in autumn at the same time as the big seedheads ripen to bronzy bladders.

Judas tree (*Cercis siliquastrum*). I'm also very keen on the Judas tree for its big round leaves, and its peculiar habit of growing masses of purply-pink pea-flowers straight out of the trunk and branches before it grows its leaves. It is also a good tree for hacking around, so you can bully it into a really craggy shape or cut it back if it gets too big, without killing it. Some that got blown over by the hurricane, years ago, are now growing back more architectural than ever.

Japanese bitter orange (*Poncirus trifoliata*) is the only hardy citrus – it's a really tough plant with leathery lemon-like leaves, cranky green stems and 2-inch spines. Given a hot summer it'll have rather unappetizing-looking 'tangerines', but I don't think you would fancy eating them.

HINT-OF-MED SHRUBS

Hebes are mostly knee-high bushy evergreen shrubs with tapering spikes of pink or purplish-blue flowers; they are at their best all summer. Really drought-tolerant. Bees love them.

Ceanothus is a very glamorous but biggish shrub that is simply smothered in blue flowers for several weeks; needs a very sunny spot with plenty of room, and loves the heat.

Californian poppy (*Romneya coulteri*) has enormous white crinkly poppy-flowers and straight six-footish stems of good greenish-grey foliage. It usually dies back to the ground each winter unless you live in a very mild area, so hack off the dead bits but don't think the whole plant's dead, because it grows back.

PLANTS TO GROW AS A KNEE-HIGH CARPET

Evergreen herbs. For an authentic taste of the Med, pile in the decorative evergreen herbs like santolina, phlomis, nepeta and artemisia, and the semi-cooking ones like rosemary, variegated thymes, lavenders and ornamental sages.

Ornamental onions (alliums) look really good poking up through a carpet of decorative herbs; these have huge spiky mauve or purple flowers, and the seedheads look even more brilliant after the flowers are over – they have strange skeletal geometric shapes like giant snowflakes. I often cut some and spray them with metallic paint to use as Christmas decorations.

Euphorbia ▶ Stunning sun-loving species include *Euphorbia wulfenii*, *E. cyparissias* and *E. mellifera*. They team well with lavenders and herbs, but all euphorbias have milky sap which is very irritant, so watch out when you are handling them.

Sea hollies. Amazing-looking perennials with metallic stems and leaves and spiky petrol-blue flowers; they mix brilliantly well with grasses.

Grasses. Great for spiky effects, the most drought-tolerant kinds are things like festuca – blue and tufty; *Stipa gigantea* – like an explosion of oats; and *Leymus arenarius* – broad blue leaves and blue 'wheat' heads.

TENDER TREES FOR YOUR PATIO TUBS

Oranges and lemons, olives and pomegranate trees are great for adding instant Mediterranean character to the patio, and now you can buy them all over the place in

pots, either as small bushes or trained into formal standard shapes. Two plants I see growing all the time in Portugal are oleander and datura, which reach tree size there – it really bugs me we can't grow them like that at home. The big drawback is that none of them are frost-hardy, so if you are going to keep them you need to keep them in pots so they stay portable and move them under cover from mid-September to the end of May. Small plants are not too bad, as you can keep them on a windowsill indoors. But big plants in tubs need putting into a heated greenhouse or sunroom, where there is more room.

GETTING DROUGHT-PROOF PLANTS GOING

People often don't realize that even the most drought-proof plants need a bit of help to get going when you first plant them. When you buy the plants, soak the roots for a couple of hours to really charge them up with water. Dig about a bucketful of bark chippings into each square metre of the soil where you are going to plant them (bark chippings last longer than manure or garden compost in dry soil), and after planting spread a layer of gravel round the plants as a mulch. By planting in autumn you can avoid having to do too much watering, but if you plant in spring or summer you need to keep new plants watered until they find their feet and can fend for themselves. Once their roots start to spread out into the soil, you shouldn't need to do any more watering.

VERTICAL INTEREST

One thing you see lots of in real Mediterranean gardens is climbers. They grow them up the walls or over a pergola on the back of the house – some of the pergolas are wonderful, with the 'roof' just made out of rough branches all tangled with knobbly grape-vines and bunches of fruit dripping down. I'm a big fan of climbers – my garden at home is full of them. In the Med they are useful for cooling the garden down, as without them the rendered walls of the villas reflect so much heat and light the gardens would be unbearable. But at home they just soften the look. I like to see a huge mish-mash of climbers all jostling for space on trellis, up walls or just shinning up into trees. They are also a great way of covering structures like an old shed or a trendy creeper-clad tunnel. Being big, climbers fill up a lot of room, so it only takes a few plants to make a garden that looks stylish but doesn't need a lot of looking after.

Think Mediterranean and say the name of the first climber that comes into your head. Grape-vines, right? Grapes make brilliant climbers for walls, arches, or on a pergola – they look good growing up rustic poles, brick pillars, or sophisticated Italian-style twisted stone columns. Anywhere so long as it's sunny. What's good about grape-vines is that they create lots of shade, and make a really lovely relaxing place to sit underneath. You can hack them back early in spring when they get too big.

And you get grapes. There are several varieties that will give you good bunches of grapes that will ripen outside so they are sweet enough to eat straight off the vine towards the end of summer. But a lot of the outdoor grapes sold are really only good for making wine, and their grapes taste a bit sour if you eat them. The one in my garden originally came from the vineyard down the road, so last year I decided to make wine from the crop. It took about ten hours of work, I made half a bottle of wine, and it tasted like dry sherry. It was great fun, but somehow I don't think Oddbins have much to worry about.

PLANTING CLIMBERS

However you use climbers at home, they are only as good as their roots – so that's why it's important to plant them properly. Climbers often have problems because the soil in the places we grow them tends to be full of builders' rubble and foundations, so you need to make better preparations than you would for just planting a shrub down the garden.

1. Dig plenty of well-rotted compost or manure into the soil, and if you are planting against a wall don't just do the place you are planting in – prepare the whole border in front of the wall so the climber has plenty of good soil to grow into. Then dig a hole, tip the plant out of its pot and put it in. Most climbers should be planted so that the top of the rootball ends up level with the surface of the surrounding soil, but if you are planting clematis put them in deeper, so that the top of the rootball is 4 to 6 inches underground. This means the plant can send out new shoots from below ground if the top gets killed off by disease or over-enthusiastic hoeing.

2. If you are planting a climber against a wall, it'll need something to grow up – it's actually easier to put up some trellis before putting the plant in (there's more on trellis in the chapter 'Contemporary Style', page 71). Tie or wind the stems around the trellis, as even self-twining climbers need help getting going.

PLANTING CLIMBERS

1

Grapes are not the only good climbers for creating a Mediterranean look. You can get some stunning ornamental vines, and other climbers too. There are loads of ways of using them. At Monet's garden in the South of France there is a big tunnel, like a dozen or so arches standing one behind another in a row, with climbers growing over each arch so the stems make big festoons like garlands looping round them. Underneath there's a gravel path with trailing nasturtiums growing out of it, almost like a reflection of what's going on overhead. It looks brilliant.

Edible grapes. Ask for 'Strawberry' or 'Leon Millot', which have full-sized grapes that ripen reliably even when you don't prune them, or 'Brandt', which has delicious mini-grapes and leaves with great autumn colour.

Purple grape. This is the one that has purple leaves and purple grapes, which are small and pippy, but edible. It doesn't really have a common name but 'purple grape' should find it at the garden centre. Or look for it under its Latin name, *Vitis vinifera* 'Purpurea'.

Ornamental vine ▼ I'm crazy about this one, which is *Vitis coignetiae*. It doesn't have grapes but it has the most enormous textured leaves that go flame red and orange in autumn, and unless you hack it back it gets huge, and makes great ropes of creeper swinging through the trees – real Tarzan stuff. A leaf makes a great plate when you are eating outdoors. Just lay one on a paper plate and put slices of cold meat or what-have-you on top – looks very rustic, and no washing up afterwards.

Yellow roses. South-of-France-style roses, like *Rosa banksia* and the giant single yellow 'Mermaid', are real sun-lovers and very spectacular, but they grow enormous and don't want any pruning, so only choose them if you have lots of room. Otherwise any yellow climbing roses would do – the yellow varieties are weaker growers than other colours and need warm sunny surroundings to do well, so they do best on a south-facing wall. Whatever you do with them, climbing roses always seem to have loads of bare stems at the bottom which makes them look a bit scraggy. I like the idea of growing morning glory up them. It hides the bald bit, and adds a more Mediterranean touch – I particularly like the combination of great big purple morning glory flowers with yellow roses.

Akebia quinata is one climber I'm quite passionate about. It's unusual enough not to have a common name. But it's brilliant – plum-tinged leaves and funny little maroon flowers you'd hardly notice, but in a warm sheltered garden and a good sunny spot you can sometimes get peculiar sausage-shaped fruit, which look great poking out of the leaves. Looks brilliant growing with grapes.

Campsis. Another real sun-lover. You often see plants for sale in garden centres but it's not worth bothering with unless you live south of Watford and have a really hot sunny spot like a south-facing wall – anywhere else and it won't flower. The variety 'Madame Galen' is the one to go for, as it is the most reliable bloomer. Given the right spot, a plant in full flower is a blaze of big orange and red trumpets – pure South of France.

THE BASICS PRACTICAL TIPS: SUPPORT FOR AND ROUTINE CARE OF CLIMBERS

Support. Most popular garden climbers climb either by twining their stems round things, or by hanging on with tendrils or leaf stalks, and these all need something to climb on – trellis or wire-netting are the usual things. Plants with stiff stems like climbing roses and many wall shrubs only need wires, which you train them along and tie at intervals. For these you need to put rows of vine eyes – like long screws with hooks at the end – into the wall about 18 inches apart, then thread horizontal wires through them. Watch out if you grow the sort of climbers that cling on by themselves using suckers or aerial roots that wedge themselves into gaps, like ivy or Virginia creeper, as they can damage dodgy brickwork or rendering.

Pruning. Gardening books make a lot of fuss about pruning climbers – if you do it properly it varies from one kind to the next and it can get very technical. But I like climbers to look natural – a bit messy – so I just tie the young stems in to encourage new plants to cover the whole wall instead of just patches of it. And I wait till they get overgrown before doing any pruning – then I just hack them back in spring. Some, like grape-vines, can be cut back quite hard, but climbing roses are best just dead-headed when they finish flowering. With most things a safe rule of thumb is just to cut enough off to leave them looking tidier – prune after flowering if it flowers before mid-June, and in spring otherwise. With grape-vines the only safe time to cut them back is in very early spring before they really start growing, or – like figs – they bleed badly and can literally die of exhaustion.

WATER FEATURES

A water feature is pure magic in a Mediterranean garden, the finishing touch that pulls paving, pots and plants together. A tinkling fountain is the perfect antidote to dust-dry air, acting as natural air-conditioning, while running water is perfect for dunking your feet in to cool off. But you don't need anything complicated or expensive. I like very natural-looking water that resembles what happens in real Mediterranean countryside or 'working' gardens. And even if you use only a tiny amount of water, it looks wonderful if it's in character.

It's no good trying to force an English-style pond into a Mediterranean-style garden, it'll never look right. To make a water feature that 'works', it is essential to go for something that takes its style from the way water actually 'happens' there for real. Imagine a real Mediterranean hillside; all arid and dusty. This is the sort of place you might find a spring welling up out of a hole in the ground or a crevice between rocks. Behind peasant farmhouses you'll often see a well with a low circular stone surround, and out in the fields you can still find big old round-bottomed terracotta pots that they once used for cooling water, just abandoned there. In smarter gardens there is often a formal fountain or some sort of trickling water feature – or even just irrigation water running down gullies. You can have a lot of fun working out ways to incorporate those types of ideas into 'authentic' water features. They'll look great with the sort of simple low-maintenance Med style that I'm so keen on.

SPIRAL TILE WATER FEATURE

A natural spring type of water feature looks good in the very simple Med-style garden described in the last few pages. But rather than just have water welling up out of the ground between rocks, as you find with a natural Mediterranean spring, I've added an architectural top for the water to spiral down to make it into more of a decorative feature. It looks impressive but it isn't as hard to do as you'd think. You need to put in an ordinary pebble pool base first (see page 151 for full instructions). To make the tile spiral you'll also want 5 hollow aluminium tent poles approximately 4 feet long, about 6 inches of wooden dowel the same diameter as the poles, a 9-inch square of lead flashing, a few gully tiles, which are a type of roofing tile, and a short length of hose. I bought second-hand tiles from an architectural salvage yard as I love their rough-and-rugged character, but you could use new ones from a builder's merchants if you prefer.

If you want to finish the feature off the way I've done it here, you'll also need half a dozen pieces of roofing slate and some suitable plants to put round the edge.

1. Start by cutting 5 hollow metal tent poles to different lengths – each one needs to be about 6 inches shorter than the last. Set the longest one aside for now. Cut the piece of dowel into 4 x 1 inch lengths and hammer them down into the top of the other 4 tubes so one end of each is tightly filled with wood. Push the 4 poles as deep as possible into the ground, with the dowel ends up. Then drill holes into the dowels.

2. These tiles already had holes, but if there aren't any you will have to drill some in order to screw them on to the uprights. It's a good idea to buy a few spare tiles in case of accidents. Put a screw through 1 tile to fix it on to the dowel on top of the first pole. Place a washer between the tile and the head of the screw to prevent the tile cracking. Repeat the same procedure with each of the 4 tiles, placing them so they slope slightly down and lead round in a gentle spiral shape with the lowest one spilling out just over the centre of the pebble pool base.

3. The water pump needs to have a few optional extras fitted to get the water up to the top of your tile spiral. Use a short length of hose to connect the water outlet at the top of the pump to the bottom of the longest tent pole. (Dip the end of the hosepipe in hot water to soften it before pushing it over the end of the metal pole. This makes it much easier to do.) The bit of hose needs to be long enough to run from the pump, which sits in the bottom of your pebble pool, to the other upright poles to complete the top storey of the tile spiral. (Sounds complicated, but it'll be quite obvious when you do it!) Dig a hole and bury the end of the pole, complete with attached bit of pipe, in the ground just behind the other uprights, and firm it well round so it stays in place.

4. Cut about 4 inches of hose, soften it in hot water the same as last time, and push it over the top of the tallest upright pole. While it is still soft, bend it over so it forms a spout. Then take a piece of lead flashing (available from builders' merchants) about 9 inches square, and use tin-snips or strong scissors to make 2 short cuts at one corner – use these flaps to wrap around the top of the pole just behind the hose spout. Bend the rest into a shape like an arum lily flower; when this is bent forward it forces the hose spout to stay pointing downwards, so that it squirts the water right down the gully along the centre of the top tile in your spiral.

5. Plug in the electrics and run the pump (don't forget the pebble pool base must be filled with water before doing this). Make sure the water is all running back into the pool base, and not splashing out all over the place, otherwise the reservoir will get emptied, which wrecks your pump. There's an adjustment 'tap' on the pump so you can alter the flow rate of the water. You can also adjust the position of some of the tiles if the water does not run down them smoothly. Leave the water running for a while so you are quite sure everything is working okay, before finishing off the surrounds.

6. You can be as inventive as you like. Here I've covered the lid of the pebble pool with some slates. And I've found a large abalone shell for the water to run into, which makes a nice tinkling sound and stops the water running off over the slates too fast. To finish off, plant a few clumps of grassy plants and some Mediterranean-looking shrubs round the feature, and maybe spread a layer of smooth pebbles all round.

5

SPIRAL TILE WATER FEATURE

6

You don't need a lot of plants to set off a feature like this as it looks so good on its own, but what I'd do is make a sea of pebbles or gravel all round the pebble pool and plant a few grasses into it. Or just use one big striking specimen of waterside plant in a container. Use one without drainage holes in the bottom and just keep it topped up with water. Don't let it freeze solid in winter.

WATERSIDE PLANTS

Spanish reed ◄ One plant I'd love to see standing next to this feature is the Spanish reed (*Arundo donax*), which is the great tall upright 'grass' with cane-like stems you see growing wild in irrigation ditches between fields in Mediterranean countries. The variegated version is really stunning, but not as hardy as the plain green one – you need to grow it in a big pot and bring it in for the winter unless you live in an incredibly mild part of the country, or just like to live dangerously.

Cyperus longus looks like the cyperus pot-plant, but is hardy and happily stands up to its neck in water.

Arrowhead (*Sagittaria japonica*) has big stunning leaves more like spearheads than arrows, and flower-stalks dotted with little triangular-ish white flowers with yellow balls of stamens in the middle in summer. Looks more tender than it is, because it's actually quite hardy stood in a few inches of water in a big container.

CARE OF WATERSIDE PLANTS

Don't be afraid to hack them back. Cut them down close to water level in the autumn when they start to die off naturally, but if they look tatty sooner, you can do the deed then – they'll simply reshoot if it's too early to die down for winter. This is the best way to freshen up jaded water's-edge plants at any time of year. If there are just a few brown leaves, take a pair of scissors and snip out the offending bits, and use your fingers to pick out any mess or rubbish that builds up in the bottom of the plants – but take care, as some of the grassy type of plants have sharp edges to their leaves that can cut your hands.

MED-STYLE WATER

* Without going to any trouble at all you could introduce water into a Med-style garden just by standing a tall wide-necked terracotta jar full of water on the patio – before the days of indoor taps they were originally used to store water for use in the house,

and when you wanted some you lowered a jug into your storage jar to fill it up. Or do as the peasants used to do to cool drinking water. They'd sink a round-bottomed amphora part-way into the ground in the shade of a tree, so the soil would act as a natural ice-bucket. This looks great standing in a sea of aromatic herbs and other drought-tolerant plants, or on its own sunk into smooth pebbles under a big gnarled tree. In both cases I'd like to float a handful of red-tinged azolla (floating fern) on top of the water, just to finish it off.

* A water feature that really took my fancy at a garden I visited on a Mediterranean holiday one year was a pergola absolutely packed with climbers till you could hardly see out. Inside, they had an irrigation pipe running right along the middle of the roof, with sprinklers every 6 feet or so. When they turned it on the temperature dropped within seconds, and the foliage looked all fresh, and the paving underneath had little pools of water in all the dips and hollows – it was just like walking through a car wash. It probably doesn't get hot enough at home to make proper use of something like that, but at the height of summer it would be great to cool off in – and a very practical way to keep any tubs and pots underneath watered, as well as the climbers.

* If your Med-style garden is based round a patio with pots, then I'd certainly go for a wall fountain. This is the sort where a jet of water squirts out of a lion's head on the wall into a tank of water. The traditional ones are made up of separate parts that you have to plumb in so they are a bit tricky to install, but the easy way is to buy one that is all in one piece – fountain, water reservoir bowl and decorative surround in one complete unit – which you just hang on the wall. There are some lovely lead ones around. Float a handful of azolla on top of the water in the bowl to make it perfect.

PERFECTLY POTTY

Terracotta pots are an essential 'scene-setting' ingredient of any Mediterranean garden. They look completely at home in a smart Tuscan-style patio garden, as well as in the more rural kind of garden with a shade tree and climbers, where you just use a few containers for decoration.

Whenever I am in Portugal I see loads of lovely pots all over the place, and when I get home I always wish I'd brought some back with me, but they take up so much room in your luggage. Genuine Mediterranean pots come in all the traditional styles, which were originally designed for particular uses. For instance, years ago when peasant farmers had to be self-sufficient, they used wide-necked terracotta jars – which their wives made – to store all sorts of home-grown produce like wine and olive oil. There are squat jars for storing cheese, and even a special jar that the fishermen used as an octopus trap. They used to lower the pot over the side of the harbour wall with a line tied to one handle; along comes the octopus and gets in because it's cool inside. Then they'd just haul it up and there's your calamari supper.

If you are shopping for pots, it's worth buying one or two good-sized pieces of terracotta with bags of character – far better than loads of odds and ends that just clutter the place up. You can get modern versions of all the old traditional Mediterranean pots today, and they are over here too, at a price. You can find places that import modern Cretan pots – they advertise in gardening magazines. I specially like their Ali-Baba jars with ripples running round the sides. You'll find people selling real old antique pots at shows, but I also like to cheat, and turn new pots into old ones for myself.

DISTRESSING POTS

I hate terracotta pots that look brand new and still have that perfect, bright orange, factory-made look about them. Weather-bleached ones have much more character. When you've been using pots for a few years, the salts from the soil and lime-scale from the water come out in patches through the sides and you get that white staining that

lots of people spend ages trying to clean off. I never bother – I like them like that. For people who like their pots a bit 'distressed', there are several ways you can make new ones look old, such as spraying them with liquid manure or diluted plant food and letting them fester in a damp ditch until they go good and green. But someone I met in Portugal has come up with a great idea. He takes new terracotta pots and puts them in the sea for two years. When he brings them out, they're covered in barnacles and encrusted with flaky white scales so they look like something dredged up from an ancient shipwreck – each one is different and looks wonderful.

To make your own pots a little more characterful, I usually recommend the yoghurt method to start mosses and lichens growing. The only time it didn't work, I'd suggested it to a customer who had just bought a big terracotta urn. I couldn't believe it when she came back and told me nothing had happened, so I said have another go. Next time she was in the garden centre, she told me she'd caught her dog licking all the yoghurt off. But normally it works perfectly.

Soak a clay pot in water, then paint the outside with runny natural yoghurt. Use one that's been lying around in the back of the fridge and has gone past its sell-by date – it won't even matter if it's already growing greeny bits, in fact it probably helps if it is. All you've got to do now is hide your pot away in a cool, damp shady spot to incubate until you like the look of it – under the hedge is perfect. The one vital thing to remember is to make sure it keeps damp – it's the combination of the damp and the biological 'starter' that does the trick.

DISTRESSING POTS

A lot of Mediterranean pots are so dramatic they don't need anything planted in them – they look good on their own, just standing in a carpet of plants or pebbles. If you are going to plant something in them, then rather than swamp them with lots of fussy annuals I'd keep to something stunning but simple. I'd grow bright, colourful but simple sun-loving plants, which are characteristic of the Med. Grow all of one kind in a container, or mix several different types together. These aren't winter-hardy, so you need either to take cuttings in August and keep them on a windowsill or to bring the whole plant inside for the winter. On the other hand it's much less hassle just to buy new plants next summer – they don't cost much.

Pelargoniums ▶ Pelargonium is the proper name for geraniums. The plain red ones with really large single flowers look the most Mediterranean to me, but you can get amazing ones with multicoloured leaves in zoned patterns.

Pineapple sage is a decorative herb whose leaves smell exactly the way pineapples taste. There's also tangerine sage, which is similar but with a sharper, more citrussy scent – both have spikes of nice bright red tubular flowers.

Gazanias have big orange or yellow daisy flowers that only open when the sun is on them, really loud and showy. Some varieties have rings round the inside of each flower in a contrasting colour.

TOP TIP

KEEPING POTS WATERED

Because they are porous, terracotta pots dry out quite quickly which is a pain if you want to grow things that need lots of water, like bedding plants, or if you are away a lot. In Portugal, Dad has lots of pots and the next-door neighbours have been doing the watering when he's not there, but now they are getting on a bit I've got him to put in a drip irrigation system. You can buy them in garden centres, specially for watering containers, using nozzles that drip water only where it's needed. When you want to water, just turn on the tap. You can automate the system completely, though, if you plug it into a timer that turns it on and off at pre-set times. It works perfectly, and I'd recommend it to anyone who is out at work, goes away at weekends or takes holidays in summer, as it makes life so much easier. In some areas the water boards make you buy a licence to use an untended hosepipe, which usually means watering systems as well as lawn sprinklers; however, they approve of drip irrigation because with a dripper in each pot the water doesn't get wasted. If you don't have enough pots to need a watering system, then mix water-retaining gel

crystals into the compost before you plant your container. These swell up and absorb 'spare' water which they release when it's needed, which means plants can last out if you don't get round to watering them on time. But do follow the instructions and don't use too much. The proper way to do it is to mix the granules with water and let them swell up first before mixing the stuff into the compost. Be careful not to overdo the dose or use the crystals dry, as they swell up inside the container after you have planted it and push all your plants out, which is exasperating, to say the least.

OTHER IDEAS

CRACKED POTS

The trouble with terracotta is that it breaks very easily. I quite like pots with a few chips missing, as the slightly distressed look makes them more natural-looking. But if you don't, and it's only a small chip out of the rim, you can rub it out with sandpaper – just enough to smooth the sharp edges so you don't notice. I know because I work in a garden centre. It works on marble mouldings too. Many's the time I've given a nymph a receding hairline to disguise the fact that she's got a bit missing.

If you get broken pots, don't throw them away because there are loads of things you can do with them. For instance, if you have a big pot that has cracked roughly in two, you can lay the halves on their side on the ground and plant them with drought-proof alpines, like sempervivums or rock pinks. Or just because it looks nice, you could arrange the bits of broken pot on a seat as if someone had just found them and put them there – messy, but a tidy sort of mess. Or just half-bury the bits in the garden with plants coming out of them, like creeping plants or grasses. You can also arrange the curved bits of pots so they make patterns, like rings within rings, which look great as 'outcrops' in a gravel path, with a few creeping thymes flowing round them. Just use your imagination!

THE BASICS

WINTER CARE OF TERRACOTTA

The big problem with terracotta is it is porous. If you leave pots planted up during the winter water soaks into the sides, expands when it freezes and cracks the pot. A lot of the more expensive terracotta that is sold here is described as frost-proof, which means it's a better quality and so less likely to crack when it freezes. Antique pots that have been used to store olive oil are the most frost-proof, as the oil soaks into the pores so water can't get in. But if you've paid a lot of money for something special – perhaps an antique or a big imported pot – it's best not to risk it. Let it dry out, and store it inside a big plastic bag or in a dry shed or garage for the winter.

CONTEMPORARY STYLE

If you are making a garden for the first time, I'd always recommend a contemporary design. Contemporary gardens are fashionable – very stylish and very simple. The less you put in them, the better they look. Don't worry if you don't know much about plants. Making a contemporary garden is all about arranging shapes. If you can arrange your living-room furniture so that you like how it looks but aren't always falling over the sofa, then you can create a contemporary garden.

The basic ingredients are hard surfaces like gravel, paving, stones or timber, and some really stunning, structural evergreen plants – the two spark each other off perfectly to give you a garden that looks great all year round. But contemporary gardens don't just look good, they are very practical too. Because you use fewer plants than in a traditional garden, this style is perfect for anyone who wants a new garden that looks finished straight away, or who does not want to spend too long looking after it. So there's more time to entertain, eat outdoors or just relax and do nothing in particular.

Once you've got the basic layout of the garden, you can have lots of fun decorating it with colour, containers and arty bits and pieces. Modern garden accessories provide lots of scope – you can use outdoor lighting, or if you like gadgets and money is no object you could have a fountain you work with a remote control, just like your TV. What I specially like is how easy it is to give a contemporary garden a new look any time you feel like it, without starting from scratch again or spending a fortune on new plants and paving. All you do is redecorate it – no big hassle.

CONTEMPORARY CONTAINER GARDEN

The secret of a contemporary container garden that looks stunning is to keep it simple. Think minimalist. Some good-quality paving and pots are enough to make a complete garden in a tiny space, but if you've got more room, just use them to create an easy-care patio. This type of garden is very practical for the gardener in a hurry because there isn't much to look after. But since there is so little to it, the right ingredients are really essential.

Paving makes a great place to put fashionable garden furniture, the latest outdoor cookery gear, and all the other trappings of comfortable outdoor entertaining, but don't wreck the effect by cluttering it up. Go for strong shapes, clean lines and tidy backgrounds, with a few simple but stylish containers. Containers are easy to look after, as you don't have all that digging, weeding and tidying up that goes with growing things in the ground. You don't have to buy expensive ones – you can just decorate ordinary pots. It's fun, and it means you can easily change the look of your garden without having to replace everything. But don't go too mad, because you've still got to water containers. And to keep the contemporary look, instead of growing lots of fussy annuals in them, go for sculptural plants like grasses, plain green trimmed box shapes or tree ferns. The effect will be twice as stunning.

TOP TIP CONTEMPORARY CONTAINERS

As a horticulturist it pains me to say this, but this is a case where the containers are more important than the plants. Budget for them being more expensive too, if you want something smart. This isn't the place to make do with battered old plastic pots, because in this sort of scheme they are not going to be hidden under masses of billowing flowers. They show. The pot is the main attraction and the plant should complement it. If you choose the right pot and the right plant, they spark each other off and look brilliant, so choose your pots first – in fact, get a whole set – as that is what sets the style. Make sure they look right with your house and paving – and even with the style of your garden furniture.

Don't just look for pots in your nearest garden centre. It's worth doing the rounds of the big shows and looking in the more contemporary gardening magazines, where you'll find unusual kinds. If you like a really modern look, stainless steel buckets like the tall upright ones florists use, and even large steel kitchen utensils, are being used quite a lot now. I prefer a more natural sort of contemporary style – like the giant verdigris snail shell 'pot' you sometimes see. This is so pretty it looks good just standing among plants and pebbles, but if you want to plant something in it, then I'd go for something that complements the shape of the shell – like a rounded tussock of blue festuca grass.

Keep it simple. Simple plants with strong shapes are the sort that will look best with contemporary containers. If your plants are over-fussy, you completely lose the effect of your stylish pot. For the same reason, it's a good idea not to mix too many plants together. For a contemporary look, I'd stick to one kind of plant per container, but make it something with a dramatic shape like a grass. That same shape could be repeated several times over so you had, say, several round tubs of different grasses, all of a

different size. Use them as a group, but space them out enough so that you can see the shape of each one separately. But I still would not have many. Three or five would be plenty – odd numbers always work best.

Grasses and sedges ◄ The evergreen kinds like festuca, pictured here, and carex are specially good for containers, as you keep your effect all year round; these make neat tussocky shapes and come in a range of colours from bright blue through greens to bronze. The variegated kinds look great. And bamboos – which are just giant grasses – are brilliant in big containers.

Spiky plants like outdoor yucca and cordyline palm are specially striking, like living architecture – some also have variegated foliage. The purple ones just look as if they are dead.

Rock plants. For smaller containers you can find drought-proof spiky rock plants like sea thrift, *Sedum spathulifolium* 'Purpureum' and sempervivum – they look like pop art shapes. If you want a bigger 'statement' you could plant them all together in a big bowl so they run into each other.

Box. If you want to go to town on shapes, then box trimmed into very neat simple topiary shapes like spheres can look great. You could just have a row of identical box balls in pots lined up along a wall or displayed on a distressed painted wall unit. Or plant a bigger container with different-sized box balls all overlapping each other to make a cloud shape.

Tree ferns. My real favourites of all are the Tasmanian tree ferns. They look prehistoric, just a thick hairy trunk with a great spray of ferny fronds sticking out of the top. In New Zealand some tree ferns are so common that they use the trunks as timber called 'punga' for making fence posts, which take root and start sprouting – a row of them wired together looks amazing, but don't go getting ideas because over here, the plants are expensive and not reliably hardy enough to risk trying it. I keep mine in a pot and move it under cover for the winter.

DIVIDING A PERENNIAL

Perennials like hostas and grasses don't usually need dividing until they are about 3 to 5 years old, depending on how fast they grow. You can always tell a plant that needs splitting up – either it becomes a solid mass of leaves and stems with very few flowers, or the middle dies out leaving healthy green shoots in a ring round the edge. Dividing rejuvenates it, so you start again with fresh new plants. But dividing is also a good way to propagate a clump-forming perennial, so some people split plants up before they need it, to make 'spares'. Spring is the best time to divide perennials.

1. Tip the plant out of the pot or dig it up from the garden and remove loose soil from the roots, then lay it down on the ground. Look for a natural division between groups of shoots, where the clump would easily separate into 2 self-contained plants. Use a long knife to carve it up, or lever it apart with a pair of garden forks used back to back.

2. Once the clump has been broken up a bit, it's quite easy to separate it into smaller pieces with your fingers. Choose the strong healthy-looking bits to re-plant, and throw away any old faded or dead-looking pieces as they'll never do any good. You can use the same technique for dividing up a congested plant growing in a pot – again spring is the best time, but with small leathery plants like this evergreen sedge you can get away with doing it in summer too, if you keep the new plants well watered afterwards.

1

DIVIDING A PERENNIAL

2

WINTER CARE FOR HARDY PLANTS IN CONTAINERS

Frost-hardy shrubs, grasses and perennials can live outside in containers all the year round. You'll still need to water them if they look dry, but not so often as in summer, and there's no need to feed them in winter. Tie tall plants up to trellis or fencing to stop them blowing over and breaking – or stand cobbles on the top of the pot for extra weight.

If pots stand in puddles when it rains, lift them up on bricks or pot feet so the plants don't 'drown'. And in long cold spells, insulate the pots so the ball of roots inside cannot freeze solid – if this happens plants can be killed, as their roots cannot take up any water. You can protect plants from freezing up by moving them into a carport or shed for a week or two – in winter they are dormant so they won't mind being in the dark for a while. Or dig a hole for each pot and sink them in soil to their rims. Another way is to tie bubble wrap plastic insulation round each pot and over the top of the compost, then drape horticultural 'fleece' (which is like a white woven insulation fabric, from garden centres) or an old curtain over the plants.

DECORATING PLANTS IN CONTAINERS WITH THINGS ON STICKS

It's great fun to decorate plants in containers by pushing things on sticks, like garden flares, moss shapes or small bird-feeders, into the pots. You can even do without plants at all – just push decorations into a stunning container filled with sand.

You can buy all sorts of decorations on sticks, but they are terribly easy to make for yourself. Use short thin bamboo canes, and cut them between the joints so you have a hollow stem. Into this push seed-heads, cut with a short stem, or use bits of copper bonsai wire twisted into a starburst shape, small Christmas tree decorations, balls of raffia with a short bit of wire pushed into them, or anything else you fancy.

I've seen some very pretty copper dishes-on-sticks, for bird-seed, that look like water-lily leaves on stalks. They look great pushed into tubs of plants, but you can make your own quite easily out of second-hand copper from a junkyard. They get it from old water tanks, so one side is a nice verdigris blue where it has been in contact with the water. Cut out the shape of large leaves using tin snips. I always take a real leaf – you don't have to use water-lilies, hostas are easier – and cut round it, as the end result always looks much more realistic than when you have just worked freehand.

DECKING

Think of a cross between a patio, a veranda and a tree house – that's a deck. The most beautiful one I've ever seen was out in New Zealand, where a lot of the houses are on hills. This particular house was really spectacular, built up on stilts and surrounded by decking suspended in mid-air that reached right over the bush. They'd cut 'windows' in the floor, covered with perspex, so you could look down on to the bush below. And right in the middle was the jacuzzi – wow.

Decking is fairly new to the UK, but in America and other parts of the world it's been *big* for years. It's very contemporary, and yet very natural because it is made of wood. It looks a bit like having a dance-floor in your garden, wonderful for walking on barefoot, but sudden death to stilettos because of the gaps. It's very adaptable – brilliant for a sloping garden, where you can make several timber terraces linked with steps, but on level ground you can build up decking on two levels to make it look more interesting. You can also cut bits out, plant through holes, build on stilts and do all sorts of things you couldn't do with a couple of tons of paving slabs if you'd chosen to have a patio instead. For the fashion-follower, decking is the hottest must-have garden ingredient. I'm crazy about it.

A brand new deck looks a bit stark, and it wants a few touches to make it sit happily with the house and garden, but don't be tempted to start cluttering it up too much. Decks look much better with just a couple of things on them: one really good container and a little arty something or other – maybe a pile of cobbles, or a glass globe, or a funky piece of bog wood. Keep it simple, and it's a lot easier to look after. For a totally maintenance-free look, I like to plant through a gap in the deck. That way, the plants are growing in properly prepared soil and virtually look after themselves. Depending on the layout of your particular deck, you could make a small sunken garden packed with plants in the middle, or banks of evergreens set in beds round the side. But my first choice would be a single tree or shrub growing through a cut-out square.

PLANTING A LARGE SPECIMEN PLANT FOR INSTANT EFFECT

There's no need to hang about waiting for small plants to grow – sometimes you really need a bigger specimen for instant impact. Big plants cost quite a bit more and can be trickier than youngsters to get going, so it's worth taking extra care to plant them properly.

1. Dig out a big planting hole, 2 or 3 times the size of the pot your plant is growing in. Mix in lots of of well-rotted garden compost, manure or tree-planting compost to improve the soil you've dug out.

2. Lift the plant out of its pot. Don't break up the rootball, but if the roots make a really solid mass gently prise a few strands away from round the edges. Otherwise they may not be able to get out into the soil.

3. Put some of your improved soil back into the hole, so that when you put the plant in, the shoulders of the rootball are level with the soil surface. With the plant in place, turn it round so its best side faces the direction you are mostly going to see it from. (It's a little cosmetic trick we use on telly all the time, but it makes all the difference in the garden too.)

4. Finally shovel more soil round it to fill up the rest of the hole, and firm it down gently with your boot. Phormiums like this one are some of my favourite feature plants. A good-sized specimen can be tucked into a border to make it look more mature in minutes, and they are good grown through gaps in decking or in big pots too.

PLANTING A LARGE SPECIMEN PLANT FOR INSTANT EFFECT

Very simple structural shapes suit the clean lines and contemporary style of decking; look for striking evergreen shrubs, a small tree with lots of character all year round, or perennials and grasses with good foliage.

Mahonia. A good evergreen for sun or shade, mahonia has holly-like leaves arranged in patterns, and the whole shrub makes interesting spiky shapes. It has starbursts of yellow flowers in winter or early spring, and some species, like *Mahonia japonica*, have a lingering lily-of-the-valley perfume. Grow it through a hole in the deck.

Birch ◄ The ultimate contemporary tree, birches make wonderful shapes without casting much shade. They have pretty yellow autumn tints and the leaves, being small, don't make a dreadful mess when they fall. In winter you see the tree at its best – the shining white trunk stands out really well against a timber background. Grow it through a hole in the deck.

Miscanthus. Forget lots of fussy little grasses, and go for a big dramatic fountain-shaped miscanthus. Gold-ringed *Miscanthus sinensis* 'Zebrinus' grows to about 6 feet, and there are other varieties with big feathery plumes rather like posh pampas grass. Grow masses of it in banks round a deck.

Perennials. Hardy ferns and hostas look great together, and between them you can get so many different foliage colours, shapes and textures: ribbon-like, lacy, round and waxy, variegated, curly – you name it. If you want plants that mix well and still give a clean-cut contemporary look, these are the ones to go for. Grow them in a sunken bed in the middle of a deck, where you look down on them.

THE BASICS

DESIGNING, BUYING AND MAKING YOUR OWN DECKING

* Don't design yourself a deck that is just a plain square or rectangle – have a bit jutting out, or leave a hole for a plant to grow up through at a strategic spot.
* Building a deck is something you could do for yourself if you are a confident DIYer. You can find the materials and instructions in most DIY suppliers these days. It's really quick compared to making a patio.
* If you aren't into DIY then it's best to get an expert in. There are all sorts of firms that specialize in doing decking, but – sorry to sound like your granny – you get what you pay for. There are decks and decks. Some decks, frankly, look like they were made out of pallets. And the sort made entirely of straight bits of wood all running in the same direction are plain boring. I know that they are easier to make and cost less as you don't waste so much of the materials, but if you are going to have a deck at all then *do* make a decent job of it.

COLOUR FOR DECKING

If you are a woody sort of person, like me, you'll probably prefer to leave decking the natural colour of the timber, though you will need to treat the surface with wood preservative so it keeps its colour and to prevent it rotting. You can also get a huge range of coloured timber treatments, which are fine if you like that sort of thing – some colours can look good in the right place – but if you go for a very jazzy effect, well, you've got to live with it.

DECKING SQUARES

Some of the decking squares you buy in DIY stores are a bit thin and lightweight to make regular decking from, though they are useful for temporary hard surfaces in all sorts of other places round the garden. They are specially brilliant in a hot dry garden, laid on gravel or pebbles to make a cool, smooth surface you can walk on without shoes.

GAZEBO

If you like to relax in your garden at the end of the day, why not treat yourself to a gazebo? Think of it as an open-air 'room' for enjoying yourself in. It's not as posh as a summerhouse, and it's not as basic as a shed. You don't keep your gardening gear in it, though you'll probably want to put garden furniture in it for the summer. It's the perfect place to sit and unwind with a bottle of wine and a bowl of olives when you get home from work on a warm summer's evening. It'll give you years of pleasure. And I bet if you get one, you'll reckon it was your best gardening buy of the year.

What I like most about a gazebo is that lovely 'home from home' feeling you get – a bit like camping in the garden. You can make it as comfy as you like. Have a seat with lots of cushions, and a pine cupboard to keep a few essentials in, like a corkscrew – and maybe insect-repellent if mozzies are a nuisance. I'd certainly want to eat out in my gazebo, so a barbecue nearby is essential. I caught the bug for campfire cooking when I was bumming around New Zealand doing a bit of apple-picking after I finished college. Over there, it was any excuse to rustle up a few lamb kebabs after work and sit up talking and drinking half the night. Now, I like to grow a few evergreen herbs like rosemary, French lavender and thyme somewhere handy, and chuck the woody herb twigs that are too tough for cooking on to the coals when they start dying down. The scent of warm herbs takes me right back to those Auckland cook-outs.

When you want to stay out after dark on a nice evening, hang a few garden lanterns with nightlights in them inside or around the gazebo. They add loads of atmosphere, which is great if you have friends round, and even better for a quiet romantic evening for two. You can also get giant garden candles, which look nice and colourful – just stick them into a border or into big containers of plants as contemporary decorations when they are not being used. But what you must have round a gazebo are some plants. I'd always grow a few big easy-care climbers over it, maybe a few pale-coloured flowers in the garden around it as they show up well at night, and just one really stunning container inside – planted with something scented, if possible.

PLANTING A HANGING BASKET

Surfinia petunias have a really strong scent which you'll notice most when they are hung up in a gazebo – the scent builds up instead of getting blown away as it does out in the open. Don't worry about the basket being under cover – unlike most bedding plants, which need lots of sun, petunias actually grow best when they get a bit of shade. Pale colours like white, cream and lilac stand out best in evening light.

1. If you buy a traditional open-sided hanging basket like this, you need to line it with a circle of black polythene with slits cut in it or a special hanging-basket liner from the garden centre, to make it hold compost. With a bought liner, all you do is drop it in, then adjust the flaps so they overlap each other to make a 'nest' shape.

2. You'll need a bag of potting compost – don't use garden soil because it isn't good enough for ultra-intensive gardening in containers. Soil-less kinds are best for filling hanging baskets as they aren't as heavy as soil-based John Innes compost, but hanging basket compost is best of all. This is soil-less compost with water-retaining granules added to stop it drying out too fast – a common problem with hanging baskets. Break down any big lumps in the compost and then half fill the basket with it.

3. Most hanging baskets have round bottoms – sit them on top of a bowl or bucket so they can't roll around while you work. Begin by putting a circle of plants in through the side of the basket. You do this by pushing the ball of roots in from the outside, and tucking them between the flaps in the liner.

4. When you've put about 6 to 8 plants in the sides, fill the basket up to the rim with compost and plant another 4 to 6 plants in the top. Although they need a bit of room to grow, I always like to cram plenty of plants into a basket so you get instant results. Water well, and you are ready to hang it up.

5. A hanging basket or two looks good round the edge of a gazebo where the plants get a bit of shade and shelter but don't get in the way of your seating area. You need a really strong, well-fixed hook to take the weight. This combination of petunias and Swan River daisies looks great and they'll keep flowering till autumn.

5

PLANTING A HANGING BASKET

CARING FOR HANGING BASKETS

There are two things you must remember to do, if hanging baskets are to last. Three at a pinch.

* Water them every day, twice if it's hot and breezy – they won't grow well if they dry out.
* Feed once a week, with any good liquid or soluble plant feed for flowering plants.
* It's also a good idea to nip off dead flower-heads any time you see some, as this keeps the plants flowering and stops the basket getting that faded look.

CONTEMPORARY CLIMBERS

Climbers look great growing up and over a gazebo. I like a big wodge of climbers mingled together like a living mosaic. For a contemporary look, don't play safe with old-fashioned plants like roses and honeysuckle – choose some of the more striking-looking climbers instead. Think about going for permanent woody climbers rather than the annual sort, because annuals need a lot of watering and a gazebo is often put at the end of the garden, a long way from the nearest tap. Here are some of my favourites, which you should find in any good garden centre:

Passionflower. A brilliant plant which climbs by holding on with tendrils so there's no need to tie it up. The flowers are very spectacular – great big saucer shapes with whiskery centres, usually in blue and white or mauvish-purple shades, and they keep coming all summer. For an evening garden, I'd choose the white variety 'Constance Elliott', which is also – unusual for passionflowers – slightly scented.

Trachelospermum asiaticum. This is perfect for a gazebo as the leaves are evergreen and the white flowers have a very strong jasmine scent. It's reasonably hardy, but not so hardy that it's worth risking in cold areas. Again, you don't need to tie it up as the stems twine round any kind of support – just give it some rustic poles, trellis, or netting.

Jasmine. Fabulous flowers for scent. I'd plant two varieties together: *Jasminum officinale*, which is really reliable and has strongly scented white flowers all summer, and *Jasminum* 'Fiona Sunrise' which has gold foliage but very few flowers. They bring out the best in each other, and they also cling on by themselves with twining stems.

Golden hop ▶ A stunning twiner with large golden leaves that grows into huge swags, draping anything it grows on. No flowers that you'd notice, or scent, just lots of great foliage. If it gets too big, just hack it back hard in spring.

AN EVENING GARDEN

There's no point in going to a lot of trouble to grow patio plants which are at their best during the day when you're stuck in the office. An evening garden can really add to your enjoyment of a gazebo. I'd just plant a mixture of night-scented flowers in a bed or a really big planter right next to the gazebo. Much less work than lots of little pots, and it'll be at its very best around dusk, making a sort of misty, ghostly garden. Go for nicotiana (tobacco plant), night-scented stocks and *Datura stramonium* if you can get it (you'll probably have to grow it yourself from seed). They all have pastel-coloured flowers that show up well in low light, but you could add other white or pale mauve flowers with strong shapes, even if they don't have any scent, to make more of a show. Go for white delphiniums (for tall upright spikes), eryngium (sea holly, for knobbly flowers and structural foliage) and gypsophila (for billowing white frothy foamy shapes) – you'll have to grow those in a bed, as they are all too big even for large containers.

ONE TO AVOID

Don't choose climbing nasturtiums close to anywhere you are going to sit – the foliage stinks if you step on it, and the plants don't really climb, only trail along the ground so you have to keep tying them up.

MAKING YOUR OWN

While there are loads of different styles of gazebos available, from cheap and cheerful to elaborate and pricey, you may feel adventurous enough to try making your own. The very cheapest and easiest kind is a simple timber structure. This will look good in any contemporary-style garden. All you need are some planed wooden posts with trellis panels nailed over them to make walls, a raised decking floor inside, and pergola poles over the top instead of a solid roof. Paint it with a wood preservative; use one with a coloured stain if you like. Personally, I love wild-looking gazebos with thatched roofs. You can make a really higgledy-piggledy one using branches instead of sawn timber uprights, and thatch it with ready-made heather or willow withy fencing panels which are available in lots of different colours. Don't worry about the rather open-plan walls of a DIY gazebo. Just grow a few climbers up them. By the time they get going, you'll have all the privacy and shelter you want.

TRELLIS

When I first took an interest in gardening, aged six, people only used trellis to grow their sweet peas up – and if you grew your sweet peas properly they hid the trellis completely. Now it is popping out of the woodwork. It's a fashion accessory – the outdoor equivalent of curtains. You don't have to watch many TV garden make-overs to see that we'd never manage without trellis. Now you can get trellis with scalloped tops, arched tops and mock classical panels you put together in a row with carved knobs on the supporting posts to make an elaborate screen. There are even curved panels, great for making a 'secret' hideaway.

You can use trellis to create all sorts of 'designer' effects instantly, or to screen off your surroundings with foliage and kid yourself you are surrounded by open countryside when you actually live in the middle of town. Round your patio or deck it is good for stopping the draughts, gives you somewhere to sunbathe out of sight of the neighbours, and is a practical way to grow climbers where you don't have any walls or soil – you can just plant them in containers. You can put up free-standing screens of trellis round the edge of the garden instead of fencing, at the back of a border to make a raised background for perennials and grasses, or across the garden as a sort of 'room divider' – all with or without climbers.

Trellis is the ideal quick-fix for all sorts of situations, and is positively brilliant for fake gardening, as you can use it to create all sorts of optical illusions. And you can still put it on the walls.

PUTTING UP TRELLIS

The solid square-patterned trellis panels are a lot stronger than the diamond sort that concertinas to various sizes – with those, you need to screw 2 battens to the wall about 5 feet apart and screw the top and bottom of the trellis to them. With the square sort, shown here, you can just screw a panel straight to the wall. Hold it in position, with the base about a foot above the ground, and drill through the wood into the wall – use a masonry drill, as you're going into bricks. To stop the drill skidding off the wood when you start, make a small dent in the wood by lightly tapping a hammer on a punch (or use a big nail) on the spot first.

REMOVABLE TRELLIS

Instead of screwing trellis to the wall, it's often a good idea to put hooks in the wall and just hang it up instead. That way, if you ever need to get at the wall – say, to paint it – or to treat a timber fence with wood preservative, you can just lift down the whole climber, trellis and all. Lay it flat on the ground, cover the plant with a sheet of plastic or a big dustsheet while you work, and then it's dead easy just to hang the whole thing back up again afterwards.

CONTEMPORARY CLIMBERS FOR TRELLIS

ANNUAL CLIMBERS

Plant these outside in late spring after the last frost, which is usually around the end of May, and pull them out when they finish flowering in autumn as they get killed by the cold. You should be able to find plants at the garden centre at planting time, but it's easy to raise your own from seed on a windowsill indoors, starting in early spring.

Purple bell vine (*Rhodochiton atrosanguineus*). This is one of my favourite annual climbers, with long dangly rather fuchsia-like flowers in purple and mauve, and stems that hold themselves on to whatever you give them for support – it looks good grown up rustic trellis. We used to grow tons of it at the Chelsea Physic Garden when I worked there, and we always pricked out lots more seedlings than we really needed, just so we could plant the 'spares' all over the place.

Chilean glory vine (*Eccremocarpus scaber*). A fast-growing annual climber with lots of tubular flowers in hot spicy firecracker colours. This also holds on to its supports without help.

Morning glory. Yes I'm biased, but they are fabulous: big saucer flowers in blue, purple and maroon shades on fast twining 'vines'. Really lovely grown on trellis.

PERENNIAL CLIMBERS

Passionflower and clematis are brilliant. Both hold on to trellis without needing to be tied up, and look very colourful.

Passionflower. The blue-flowered *Passiflora caerulea* makes a great plant for a tub, and sometimes has big orange egg-like fruit after a hot summer. They aren't particularly good to eat, though they *are* a kind of passionfruit so you can try if you like – they aren't harmful.

Clematis ▼ Grow one of the smaller-growing varieties that flower in summer (look at the label). Besides being in bloom right when you want them, this also means you can cut them back hard each year in early spring, which stops lots of dead twiggy stems building up on the trellis as you just clear the whole lot away once a year. I'd go for *Clematis florida* 'Alba Plena', which has great big greeny-white rosette flowers in midsummer. If you want a big clematis that doesn't need pruning until it gets too big, go for one of the species like *Clematis tangutica,* pictured here.

TRELLIS FOR DIFFICULT SITUATIONS

* Tiny enclosed garden. If your garden is small, dark and surrounded by high walls so you don't have much of a view, why not simply create your own? I know a garden like that where the owner painted a Mediterranean scene with orange trees on the wall and used a few pieces of cut-away trellis to give it a bit of depth, as if you were looking down off your balcony out over a sun-kissed hillside. You might almost have been in Tuscany, and the sun never stopped shining.

* Long dark narrow passageway between buildings. Another common problem with a lot of town gardens is when they have a long narrow passageway between buildings leading to the back door, where there is hardly enough room to walk, let alone do anything decorative like make a garden. This is the perfect place for trellis. It adds interest without taking up space or making any work. You could use a frieze of 'classical' trellis painted a contrasting colour to the wall. Or go very simple and hang up a wall basket of ivy with a two-dimensional topiary frame just above it, to train it round.

GROWING CLIMBERS ON FREE-STANDING TRELLIS PLANT SUPPORTS

It's very trendy right now to grow annual climbers or a clematis in a border over a twiggy plant support. It's a good way to add a bit of height to a new border, and if you buy a biggish climber that's already in flower the effect is instant.

1. When you buy a climber this size that's already in flower, it's quite a job disentangling it from the canes the nursery grew it up – but you need to do it.
2. Separate the individual stems out as much as possible, trying not to break them.
3. Dig a hole about twice the size of the pot the plant is growing in, and mix some compost into the bottom of it. Tip the plant carefully out of its pot and stand it in the hole.
4. Open out your twiggy plant support – this one concertinas shut for easy transport, so you need to make sure it's expanded as much as possible. Then stand it over the plant. Spread the stems out well so they cover the framework and tie them in place.

GROWING CLIMBERS ON FREE-STANDING TRELLIS PLANT SUPPORTS

TRICKS WITH TRELLIS

Perspective trellis is a lot of fun. I've seen tiny gardens with a winding path leading down to what looks like an alcove with an urn in it at the far end, but when you get there you find the alcove and urn are just flat 'trellis tricks' screwed to the wall to make the garden look deeper than it really is. Being a planty sort of person, I'd stand a trough of trimmed box at the bottom of the trellis to add to the illusion. One of the trellis firms makes a whole range of silhouettes – Italian poplars, cherubs, bushy-topped trees, balustrades, urns full of flowers, you name it. You could just use one or two to put a bit of detail on to a plain wall, or go to town and combine lots of them with trellis panels to create a wonderful 'wall-scape' garden where you never have to do a moment's weeding or watering. A two-dimensional garden would be very different and great fun, rather like a 1940s black and white Hollywood film set.

IT'S ALL DONE WITH MIRRORS

Mirrors are a great way of making a small garden look bigger or a dark area look brighter. One of the best ways of using mirrors is behind trellis, where nobody can accidentally walk into them. They work well with normal oblong trellis panels, wreathed with climbers, on a wall or as part of a screen dividing up a garden.

You have to be quite careful where you put mirrors so that they only reflect plants, as it's very off-putting if you see yourself in them. Set mirrors at an angle behind plants so it looks as if the border goes on for ever, or use them behind an arch, turning it into a tunnel. Don't put one in an alcove so it reflects an urn or a statue, as it just looks wrong – you wouldn't really have two of them next to each other.

MAKING YOUR OWN

You can buy the usual diamond and square trellis everywhere, but if you want something a bit heavier-grade or in different patterns it's very easy to make your own, using bundles of roofing laths from builders' merchants. We do it all the time on the programme. To start with we used to use a hammer and nails – make sure you get the right length of nails as you don't want sharp points sticking out through the back – but it's much easier to use a gas nail gun. It's like using a cap pistol, you just go pop, pop, pop, and the job's done. I made some sunray-shaped trellis which was fun. You can try any shape you like.

RUSTIC-LOOK TRELLIS

My favourite sort of trellis is rustic-style. And while you can buy ready-made panels of willow wands or woven hazel, you could also try making your own rustic trellis. I saw some wonderful trellis in Italy made of rustic poles with dried grape-vine wound through it, so I thought I'd have a go at making some. I saved up the prunings off the grape-vine on my pergola, and when they were almost dry I just wound the stems through some ordinary trellis I'd bought from a DIY store. It made a tremendous difference. Another time, I'd use three really good trellis panels with arched tops, weave some vine prunings randomly through them, and then hinge the panels together to make a portable patio screen. Very trendy.

Remember, when you are using materials you've grown yourself – especially when they are things like prunings that would normally go to waste – you've got nothing to lose if it doesn't work out. So give it a go.

OUTDOOR LIGHTING

Lighting really brings a garden to life, but you don't have to wait till after dark to enjoy it. The best time to appreciate the twinkle of lights among plants is towards dusk, and there's nothing like candles for putting you in the mood when you are eating outdoors or just relaxing over a glass of wine after work.

There's more to garden lighting than just sitting out late on balmy summer nights – though that sounds pretty good to me. If you have a beautiful water feature, underwater lighting makes it mega-glamorous. You could light up your garden's best features, or have a working antique gas-mantle to welcome you home. For après-barbecue ambience, low lights outline the whole garden with a romantic glow, leading visitors safely round rambling paths and illuminating steps or drawing you to the gazebo down the garden – it's not only moths that are attracted to light.

But it's not just guests who benefit – the right lighting makes every evening outdoors into a special occasion. Try rearranging the lights slightly from season to season, or from party to party. After dark, the effect is as good as a garden make-over, but without the bother.

PUTTING IN OUTDOOR LIGHTS

Electricity gives you the greatest scope for serious garden lighting, and you can be quite artistic with it. Low-voltage kits are the safest if you are going to go the DIY route. You can get kits that run one underwater light and a couple of spotlights, which are good in a small garden with a water feature. Use the underwater light to pick out moving water, at the bottom of a waterfall or underneath a fountain, as that's where you'll get most of your sparkle. Use the spotlights to pick out one particular feature like a statue or an urn, and another to shine up into a tree. Don't floodlight the whole pond or it'll end up looking like a Beverly Hills swimming-pool.

1. Fit the spotlights on to the short spikes provided.
2. Lay the lights out where you want them to go. Thread the electric cable supplied with the lighting system through conduit (you can use garden hosepipe). Starting at the house by the place you plan to plug in, run the cable from one light to the next, going round the edge of beds, under paving or decking – anywhere it's out of sight and unlikely to get damaged. To connect to the power supply, drill through the wall into a garage, sunroom or an outside wall of the house, close to a power point. Choose somewhere you won't mind seeing a box of electrics, as there is also a small transformer to find room for. If you are worried about doing this, get a builder or electrician to do it for you. Thread the cable through the wall and fix a 3-pin plug on the other side. Plug it into a circuit-breaker, then even if anything happens to the cable you won't get a shock. When everything is connected up, switch on.
3. The spotlights have clip-on connectors you just snap into the cable to link them to the power supply.
4. Push the spotlight spikes firmly into their final position and angle them where you want them to shine.

PUTTING IN OUTDOOR LIGHTS

Globe lights. Glass globes on short stems, good low-lights for lighting up patio and barbecue areas as the soft light glows out evenly all round.

Shaded lights. Lamps with a mushroom shape that throws a soft light down to make a circle of light, useful in low-planted borders.

Pathway markers. Short squat lights that shine to one side, good for low-lighting steps. Or use small tiered lights on short stems for outlining paths.

Feature lights. Low-power spotlights that give subtle rather than striking effects – the low-voltage versions are particularly soft. They can be bought on brackets to mount on walls, or on spikes to push into the ground.

Floodlights ▼ Strong lights that need mains current for flooding large areas or for dramatic directional effects. Dramatic floodlighting can make a contemporary garden look incredibly theatrical at night. Use it to accentuate the shapes of striking plants, like a group of spiky yuccas, a twisted tree or a large-leaved shrub like a fatsia – just angle a floodlight at them. Floodlights work well with bold architectural shapes too, used along a balustrade, or at one side of a group of standing stones in a gravel garden. The sci-fi effects are all due to the contrasts between the bright light on the leaves or stone and

the long dark jagged shadows they cast. But don't fall out with your neighbours – adjust your floodlights so they aren't shining in through their windows.

Outdoor fairy lights. In my garden I've put fairy lights up inside the pergola. Mine are the all-white version of outdoor Christmas lights, which I've dotted round in the roof where the foliage is thickest, so they look like stars twinkling through the leaves. I've arranged one string to make my horoscope constellation – Leo. Not that I believe in horoscopes, though a large unexpected cheque might convince me. One of these days when I feel in a holiday mood, I'll rearrange them as the Southern Cross – one of those coconut-scented candles and a drink with a parasol in it, and it's hallo Fiji!

ELECTRICAL SAFETY

The safest lights for outdoor use are low-voltage kits where the mains current is stepped down by a transformer, but you need to be fairly close to the house so you can plug into the power as you can't extend the cable. Even with low-voltage lights you should still plug them into a circuit-breaker, which cuts the power at once and stops you getting a shock if the cable gets cut. The big advantage of low-voltage lights is they are easy to put in for amateurs. If you want a more powerful system, for instance to run floodlights or security lighting down the garden, you need to get a qualified electrician to do the wiring and use armoured cable which has to be buried about 2 feet deep.

If you have a lot of garden electrics, like pond pumps and fountains as well as lighting, it may be worth asking about an outdoor electricity supply, which looks like a box you can plug outdoor-grade plugs into – the lid then seals down around them so no moisture can get in.

SOLAR LIGHTING

Where there isn't a power source, you can still have electric lights if you choose the solar-powered sort. These are very popular, as they are so easy to use. You don't have to think about where to run cables, or face the bother of drilling a hole in the wall to get to a power point. Just put them wherever you fancy, and any time you think of a better spot they take only minutes to move.

* Cheat and cheerful. At its simplest, you can easily create a solar starlit effect just by using those glow-in-the-dark stars that children put up in their bedrooms. They charge themselves up during the day, and when you go down to your gazebo in the evening, there are your stars. You need to make your stellar scene at night; charge the stars by shining a torch on them, then just stick them on. It's good fun, and keeps the neighbours guessing.

* Sun fun. There's a big range of proper solar-powered garden lights too. They cost a bit more than the electric type but they are so much quicker to install. You'd think they would need a sunny day to charge themselves up but not so – they work perfectly well even after a grey, overcast day. The individual lamps are not over-powerful, but they give a constant subtle glow, good for low-lighting paths and steps, or just for picking out the shape of the garden so you get the feel of it every time you look. This type of lighting normally comes on automatically at dusk and goes off again at dawn, though you can usually override the self-switching system.

CANDLES FOR SOFT ROMANTIC LIGHTING

I love candles in the garden. The very simplest ideas can look stunning. Some friends of mine have got a gorgeous wild area down the garden with a natural pond and a seat half-hidden in long grass. I'd seen it several times in daylight – but when I went round in the evening it was alive with tiny flickering lights. Very romantic, like fireflies in the twilight. It was all done using candles in jam-jars, each with a few pebbles in the bottom, dotted around on the ground. You could use drinking glasses instead.

Candles are brilliant on the patio too. They give a nice soft light which is very flattering across a dining table – everyone looks so much prettier by candlelight. You can get scented candles in half-coconut-shell holders for the table, and long wax 'flares' that look good pushed into a tub of sand. Flares usually stay lit in a light breeze, but for candles there are garden lanterns ranging from the tin-gothic sort you hang from a hook, to glass globes that dangle from metal 'shepherd's crooks' pushed into the lawn.

TOP TIP

MIDGES

If you are going to sit out at night, especially if you are near water, be prepared for midges. I have a major problem, as I live on the river. When I say on the river, I mean literally right over it – the River Test runs under the house, which was once the mill cottage, as well as round it. I'm always telling customers in the garden centre to put fish into their pond to keep mosquito larvae under control, but here it's so bad even the trout can't seem to keep on top of the problem. You can burn citronella candles, which are supposed to ward off biting insects. They smell nice anyway. But the best remedy I've found is one of those electric insect zappers, the outdoor version of the sort with the blue light you see in butchers' shops, which you hang up close to where you are sitting. All you get is the occasional sound of frying fly.

STONE AND TIMBER FEATURES

You've only got to say 'contemporary garden' for most people to think of a sort of lunar landscape of steel, concrete and glass, which looks very dramatic in a show garden but is maybe not the sort of thing you'd want to wake up to every day. At home, you can create a contemporary look that's much easier to live with using natural stone and wood. Railway sleepers, bamboo poles, hardwood decks, pebbles and paving always go well with plants – you can't go wrong. When making a contemporary-style garden, the trick is to put the hardware in first to establish the basic shape of your garden. Then decorate it with structural plants – a few striking evergreens like pines with a nice windswept character, but not too many, or you lose the shape of your scheme. To stop it looking too stark, it's a good idea to have the occasional carpet of low spreading plants to cover the ground, but keep them in well-defined areas. This gives you a stylish garden that looks good all year round. It's affordable, and easy to maintain so you have time to enjoy it. Best of all, it's instant. You can cut out most of the weeding for months or even years to come, just by keeping the soil covered up.

MULCHING WITH GRAVEL, PEBBLES OR BARK CHIPPINGS

Mulching is a good gardening habit to get into. All it means is spreading a layer of something over the soil. You can use garden compost or manure, but I prefer gravel, pebbles or bark chippings as they last a lot longer. I like bark chippings best in a wild or woody area, and gravel or pebbles in a sunny or dry-type garden or round a water feature, but it's up to you. The idea of a mulch is not just to make the plants look good, which it does, it also keeps the soil round their roots cool and moist, and it stops annual weeds coming up. So though it takes time and money, mulching saves lots of work later. The best time to mulch is straight after planting, when you are making a new bed using trees and shrubs, perennials and grasses or rock plants, but you can mulch existing beds as long as the soil is moist and free of weeds before you start. Just spread the material out in an even layer all over the ground, tucking it under low-growing or spreading plants. A mulch needs to be 2 inches deep to really work well. Perennial plants and bulbs can push their way up through it every year when they start growing, but so can perennial weeds like nettles and bindweed, so don't imagine you'll never need do any weeding again – but a mulch will stop annual weeds by keeping their seeds in the dark so they can't germinate. You'll need to top up a mulch of bark chippings every spring or autumn when you tidy your borders, because bark slowly breaks down and the worms pull it into the soil (which is good for the ground), but gravel and pebbles last for years – when they start to sink in, just top up with another thin layer. With mulching, the bigger the 'bits' the longer they last!

MULCHING WITH GRAVEL, PEBBLES OR BARK CHIPPINGS

SEASIDE-STYLE GARDENS

It's almost impossible to have too much gravel or too many pebbles in a garden. If you are worried it's going to end up looking like a beach, don't – seaside gardens look great inland too. They are the ultimate in low maintenance, as you don't need much in them. Just a few bits of flotsam – anything that looks like it could have been washed up by the tide. You can cheat and use old railway sleepers or scaffolding planks that have gone a bit rotten in places. Just hack out the soft bits, treat with wood preservative, then half-bury the timber in pebbles. For plants, go for fairly rugged kinds that look the part and won't give you any trouble. Always do the planting last – but don't do too much. What looks good in this sort of garden is a pine tree, but you want one with a slightly windswept shape. Look for a lopsided one in a garden centre; they aren't hard to find as everybody always wants a perfect symmetrical one and the bent ones get left till last. I'd plant an upright craggy sort of shape next to one that clings to the ground to create a naturally windswept look.

ALL ABOUT STONES

* If anyone else asks me what I think about people pinching pebbles off the beach . . . aarrgh! Don't do it. The pebbles and cobbles that they sell in bags in the garden centres are perfectly legally mined from underground; they don't come from the beach at all. They are a by-product of the building business. When aggregate is extracted for road-building, they sort out the pebbles and cobbles, bag them, and sell them for gardeners. If we didn't use them, they'd only end up as aggregate too.

* If you want chunkier rocks, look in an architectural salvage yard or a reclamation centre, as they often have second-hand stones from old rockeries.

* It's amazing what you can find just by digging around in your own garden. At one garden in Yorkshire we made-over for a programme I found the most wonderful bits of stone just by getting the borders ready for planting. The trouble was that by the time I'd dug it all out to make a rockery, the soil level had dropped about 4 inches.

If you go for a minimalist sort of garden, you don't have many plants, so make sure the few you do have are big and bold so you can't miss them. You might see a single really craggy windswept pine, a group of junipers, or an angular conifer – one of those weird weeping forms that looks like a drunk leaning up against a lamp-post. If you like a slightly softer effect, you could make a carpet of hillocky, spiky and aromatic plants, growing in groups out of a mulch of gravel or bark chippings.

Willow ▼ A clump of silvery or white-leaved willow stems (such as *Salix exigua*, pictured here) takes up a lot of space and looks very sculptural, but apart from chopping it off close to the ground every spring it doesn't make any work.

Tamarix. A real seaside tree, with feathery foliage and sprays of tiny pink flowers in summer. This is another one you can hack back to give it a craggier shape and stop it growing too big as it gets older.

Prostrate junipers. These are the sort that naturally grow clinging close to the ground. You can get various shades of green, blue-green and grey, also sprawling semi-prostrate sorts with gold highlights. In the garden centre, look for *Juniperus horizontalis* or *Juniperus* x *media* varieties.

***Pinus nigra* 'Maritima'.** Another real seaside tree that naturally grows into a craggy windswept shape and doesn't mind drying winds or dry soil – two things most conifers hate.

Yucca filamentosa. Makes a great green spiky shape like a mega-pineapple top, and periodically flowers producing a tall upright stem loaded with what look like lots of small white lightbulbs. Very dramatic.

FUN WITH STONE

In America you sometimes see 'stone gardens' which are very contemporary and have only a few really structural plants. All the detail comes from great sweeps of different-sized stones and gravels that make great swirling textured patterns.

* Stone statements. They could be lumps of rock, piles of pebbles, or big cobbles, so long as they are strategically placed – or, as the arty set would say, 'making a statement'.

* Monoliths. I'm very keen on monoliths – anything from a single standing stone to your own mini-Stonehenge. If you have the sort of garden where you're always digging up bits of slate or you're trying to re-home stray chunks of rock from an old rockery, then this is a good way to use them. Clean them off, or for a wilder look use them just the way you found them – moss, muck and all.

* Pebbly pyramid. Pebbles and cobbles are brilliant for garden ornaments. Big cobbles look good piled up, or you can paint things on them, like flowers or the name of your house. You can buy pebbles that have been drilled through the middle – buy the smaller ones and thread them on to bent metal pipes, or just drop them over a short pole hammered into the ground, with the biggest ones at the bottom so they make a pebbly pyramid. The good thing about this is that once you have some pretty stones, you can keep re-using them in different ways.

WOOD 'SCULPTURES'

If you want a bit of natural sculpture, use an old tree stump. You can sometimes buy ones that have been sandblasted, though untreated natural ones look good too – and if you know someone who is having a tree stump winched out of their garden, bag it! You could even just throw a pile of logs together in a heap. It doesn't have to be anything too clever – and anyway, you can always enhance your creation with a few good spreading plants or a sprawling climber. The effect is supposed to be casual.

A timber version of a monolith can also look brilliant: just stand a chunky bit of timber up on end. You could chop chunks out of a thick pole to turn it into a kind of wild totem-pole. I've seen a Canadian garden with a group of five real fierce-looking, hawk-nosed red and blue totem-poles glaring out over a carpet of plain green foliage, which looks great – and there's nothing to maintain.

ON THE WILD SIDE

Natural-looking gardens are terribly popular now. They are fashionable, wildlife-friendly and practical, ideal for the not-so-tidy sort of person or for anyone who's too busy for a fussy kind of garden.

At the water garden centre where I work, the semi-wild look suits us perfectly and tends to happen on its own, as there's only me and two others to look after two acres. We get lots of self-sown wildflowers like poppies and foxgloves, and seedlings of things like perennial sweet pea, all mingling with the plants we originally put in.

This mixture of wild and tame plants is a paradise for wildlife. We have wrens and tree creepers, and because of the river there are kingfishers, bats – which are attracted to the midges on the water in the evening – and trout, as well as all the usual garden wildlife like frogs, newts and hedgehogs. It looks wonderful, not quite conventional gardening but not totally wild either.

You can be quite arty with this sort of garden too. There are loads of decorative things you can make out of plant stems and seed-pods to jazz things up without losing the natural style. At one garden, we built a very natural-looking gazebo with a lovely woven hazel window-box outside. I rehung the window-box on the inside of the gazebo, just under the window. There wasn't enough room for a table in there, but this window-box was just the right size to take a bottle of wine, a couple of glasses and a packet of crisps. Wild gardening is great, but there's no point in roughing it, is there?

WAYS WITH WILDFLOWERS

I'm always amazed how colourful a lot of wildflowers are. Birds and animals wear their own camouflage kit so they blend into the background, but wildflowers really stand out. Some of them have such bright colours you would think they must have been deliberately bred that way. Think of campion, poppies and lythrum – hot stuff. There are some very striking shapes too, like foxgloves and ox-eye daisy. This enormous range of characters makes wildflowers good mixers. You can grow them in grass, in borders with other plants and under trees, as well as in a real patch of wild garden. There are wildflowers to suit just about any situation, so you can create little mini nature reserves wherever there's a suitable spot. You could even pop a few cowslips or primroses into a tub. The only rule with natural gardening is don't be too tidy – if you are, you'll just be taking away a valuable habitat for other wildlife. It's a great cop-out for busy gardeners, too.

GROWING WILDFLOWERS FROM SEED

You often see mixed packets of wildflower seeds on sale in garden centres. Mixtures are fine if you are sowing a wildflower meadow, but when you want pot-grown plants to put in a border or in holes cut out of existing grass, it's much better to buy packets of separate species. Apart from letting you choose which flowers you really want, growing each kind on its own is much more practical because some wildflowers germinate straight away while others take months to come up. There is no 'best' sowing time that suits them all, so read the instructions on the packet, but you can use the same method for them all.

1. Fill several small pots with seed compost and flatten the surface slightly. Then tip the packet of seed out into the palm of your hand.
2. Because the seeds are so small, don't sprinkle them by hand. The way I find works best is just to tap a finger against the side of the hand holding the seeds, so that they trickle out in a very fine stream over the compost. That way, all the seedlings will be nicely spaced out when they come up and you won't have to spend ages trying to separate them, which usually means that loads of them get broken.
3. The seeds need to be covered with a tiny amount of compost – it's only supposed to be as thick as the actual width of the seeds. An ordinary kitchen sieve has holes

that are too small to let any compost go through, so just use another pot with small drainage holes in the bottom as your sieve. Half fill the pot and tap it gently to let some compost go through the holes.

4. Instead of watering the pots with a watering-can, which would just wash half the contents out, stand them in a dish of water for 5 minutes. That's long enough for the water to damp the compost from the bottom up, which doesn't disturb the seeds. Label each pot so you know what they are, then stand them in a shady place outside where they won't get knocked over. Water them the same way each time the compost starts to dry out. When the seedlings are big enough to handle, plant them all into small pots of their own and keep them growing somewhere safe until they are big enough to plant in the garden.

GROWING WILDFLOWERS FROM SEED

WOODLAND-STYLE WILDFLOWERS

I love wild woodland: the dappled effect you get under the canopy of leaves, the coolness, and the contrasting areas of light and shade. And I love all the mushrooms and mossy bits of wood that go with it. Living on the edge of the New Forest, I get lots of my best ideas for natural woody-style gardens from nature itself. Anyway, it's a great excuse for just going off walking when I ought to be doing something else.

* Create a dingly-dell effect under existing trees by putting in a few shade-loving plants like wild daffodils, bluebells or foxgloves, with long grass and a nice gnarled log to sit on.
* If you don't have any trees, plant a birch, as it looks wild without casting too much shade, and grow hardy cyclamen and clumps of snowdrops in the grass around it if there's not enough room for taller wildflowers.

WHERE TO PUT WILDFLOWERS

I love the sort of borders we've got at work, where wildflowers scramble up among cultivated plants, and I love wildflower meadows at big country gardens, with short paths mown through long flower-studded grass. But you don't need a huge garden. You can tuck wildflowers into a quiet corner of the garden in a border or under trees, or you can just let them come up in your lawn. If you have lots of wildflowers growing in the countryside all round you, they'll come up naturally if you don't weed too thoroughly. But if you are introducing them, it's best to get them in pots and actually plant them – just scattering seeds around doesn't work very well.

* In borders. The bigger, brighter wildflowers like lythrum, foxgloves and campion look great in groups, dotted in between shrubs. Rosebay willowherb and ox-eye daisy look good grown in big groups. In a smaller border, wildflowers mix well with cultivated grasses – this has a very softening effect on the garden. Choose grasses with good foliage like gardener's garters, or stunning seedheads like quaking grass, which is semi-wild anyway.
* In the lawn. If you just stop mowing so much, and let the grass grow an inch or two longer than usual, you'll soon have a pretty patchwork of clover, self-heal and speedwell. But if you want other species, buy plants and put them into holes cut into the turf. Violets, cowslips and primroses are good to have running through your lawn. My grandad has loads which he planted in his borders but they've 'crept' into the lawn. After flowering, don't cut the dead-heads off too soon – leave them to shed their seeds. This way, you only need a few plants to start a thriving colony.
* Wildflower meadows. Great for picnics, a small patch of wildflower meadow at the bottom of the garden looks brilliant. Plant a few pots of tall flowers like ox-eye daisy and campion, or the old-fashioned hayfield species like corn cockle and poppies, into

existing lawn and then just let it grow. A wildflower meadow mostly looks after itself. You don't feed it, or water it, or weed it. Mow it once in late summer, after the flowers have shed their seeds, and again in early spring if you must. One thing you must do is cart the hay off the field – this removes nutrients from the soil, so the wildflowers grow stronger but the grass doesn't.

GETTING WILDFLOWERS GOING

People often think having a wild garden means just letting it run totally wild. All that does is give you a great big patch of brambles – the rabbits will love it. With a natural-style garden, you still have to do a bit of gardening. It's just that there's a lot less of it, and it's a slightly different sort of gardening than in a 'proper' garden. There are just four things to remember.

* Wildflowers don't like growing in rich garden soil, they need poor ground without any chemicals. If you are making a new wildflower lawn or meadow, just dig the ground over – there's no need for any compost or manure or fertilizer – and sow the seed evenly all over the area, like sowing a normal lawn. (You can buy mixtures of wildflower and grass seed for various situations.)

* If you want to plant wildflowers into an existing garden border, it won't matter if you have previously used fertilizer on the spot but stop using it now – and pesticides too.

* When introducing wildflowers to the garden, it's always best to put plants in. Sprinkling packets of wildflower seeds about never works. Once your first batch of wildflowers has flowered, leave them to shed their seed and from then on they'll just arrive – all you do then is weed out the ones you don't want.

* Leave the garden looking very natural, and leave seedlings of your favourite plants to grow wherever they turn up, but do pull out things like tree seedlings, brambles and fast-growing perennial weeds while they are small, because if you don't they'll take over.

WILDLIFE-FRIENDLY FLOWERS

Any wild garden really must have a few plants to attract wildlife; some kinds are particularly good at doing this.

Caterpillar plants. Have one patch of stinging nettles for the sake of the butterflies; four different kinds of caterpillars feed on them. But there's no need to go mad. I went to visit someone's wildflower meadow the other day and they said, 'We're leaving the stinging nettles for the butterflies.' Nettles being what they are, they had spread and were taking up half the garden.

Bird plants. Grow teasels, grasses and thistles, and leave the seed-heads in autumn as they attract swarms of finches to feed. Sunflowers, apples and fennel seed-heads draw a lot of birds too.

Butterfly plants ◄ For genuine wildflowers grow honesty, hemp agrimony and field scabious, but buddleia, lythrum, pictured, candytuft, and herbs like lavender and marjoram actually bring in a lot more butterflies.

Bee plants. Heathers, lavender and most of the old-fashioned hardy annuals are great for bees.

MAKING A BARK CHIPPING PATH

One thing I'd want in any wildflower area is easy access. It's not like a 'polite' garden, where there's short grass or paving between beds to keep your feet clean. With wildflowers you tend to grow them in great swathes, so you want a way of walking through without having to change into waders each time you want a quick look. A natural bark chipping path suits a wild garden perfectly. An angled path, running diagonally through a sea of wildflowers or crossing a wildflower meadow, adds a slightly contemporary slant to an otherwise very natural feature. If you have a garden with a lot of trees, you can make it feel deliciously woodlandy by making a wandering path of bark edged with fallen logs. White birch logs look lovely, but the sort you can buy to burn on the fire in winter will do fine. Buy bags of bark chippings from garden centres. I love the resinous scent when you walk on them – really yum.

1. Mark out the shape of your path and dig out the turf to a depth of 3 inches. This gets rid of all the roots, so you shouldn't have grass growing up through the path later.
2. Fork the soil over and pick out any roots of perennial weeds like docks and nettles. Tread the soil down firmly.
3. Tidy the edges where the turf has been removed.
4. Put wooden shuttering along the sides of the path, pressed up tight against the edge of the turf. You need to make a firm edge to a bark path when it runs through grass, otherwise the two have a nasty habit of creeping into each other.
5. Hammer short wooden pegs in every so often along the edge of the shuttering to keep it firmly in position.
6. Tip out bags of chippings on to your path and rake them out evenly so they are at least 2 inches deep. You don't need to put anti-weed fabric down under a path like this: it always ends up showing through, which looks awful. If you use enough depth of chippings, weeds shouldn't be a problem.

MAKING A BARK CHIPPING PATH

WILLOW AND HAZEL TWIG ART

You wouldn't want to keep the same old decorations in your house for years on end, so why put up with the same garden accessories for ever? I like gardens to change. It keeps them looking much more vibrant – and you don't have to replant the whole garden to give that impression. That's why I'm so keen on twiggy arts and crafts. There are tons of ready-made things you can buy: almost any garden centre has tripod-type plant supports for climbers, mini hurdles you just push in to prop up a floppy plant, and wicker baskets (if you want to plant things in them, they last longer if you line them with a plastic carrier bag first). There's all kinds of fencing – I got some willow screening the other day made of natural willow with the bark left on, which came in the most amazing colours from golden yellows to pinks and russet browns. You can buy fabulous heather panels, and ready-made garden sculptures made from willow stems twisted round into flowing shapes, such as grazing geese or deer.

But it's much more fun to make your own. And any time you get fed up with your present 'twig art' you can give it an after-life by using it as a natural topiary frame and planting ivy over it. When you make things for yourself, especially if you use things you have grown which don't cost you a penny, you don't mind having something that lasts only a year or two. Willow and hazel are the classic craft plants, but several smaller shrubs can be used too – or you can buy bundles of willow wands ready to use. You don't have to be terribly artistic, just play around with them until you end up with something you like.

A rustic wigwam looks great on its own in a border, and it's brilliant for growing climbers up. A basic one is very easy to make – all you do is push some straight sticks in to form a circle and tie the stems together at the top. I'd start with something quite simple first, but you can also develop the idea into something a bit more adventurous.

1. Use any long straight stems like hazel, willow or dogwood from the garden – they need to be at least finger-thick at the base – or you can buy bundles of coloured willow wands from trendy interior décor shops.
2. Mark out a circle about 2 feet across in the soil, and push several small bundles of stems in round the edge.
3. Hold each bundle of stems round the top and tie them together to make a stronger structure.
4. I always use tarred twine because I love the smell. You can get it in ship's chandlers, but you sometimes find it in DIY shops. After tying your knot, leave short trailing ends for a more rustic look.

5. When each of your bundles is tied at the top, take some long bendy pieces of stem and weave them in and out – just like making a basket. The idea is to make a firm band of woven willow round the bottom to hold the structure in shape, as well as giving climbers a leg up later. When that's finished, make a second band higher up.
6. Plant a climber at the foot of one of the 'legs'. I've used a jasmine with golden foliage called 'Fiona Sunrise' – it has scented white flowers. To make it cover the wigwam straight away, untie it from the cane it was growing up at the garden centre, spread the stems out over the uprights, then tie them loosely to the structure with twine.
7. If you don't mind the wait, one jasmine would cover this wigwam by the end of the summer – but I like quick results so I've added a couple of ivies too. Being evergreen, they'll keep the wigwam looking good in winter.

5

6

MAKING A RUSTIC PLANT SUPPORT

7

Willow (*Salix* species). At the water garden centre, we grow pussy-willows along the river because the roots help to hold the banks together. They get coppiced every three years to stop them growing too big. After they have been cut down, the stumps throw up lots of very strong straight shoots like the ones people use for making baskets. You don't need a river to grow willows though – there are some really pretty smaller kinds with coloured bark that you can grow in a normal garden. *Salix alba* 'Chermesina' (scarlet willow) is very pretty – the young stems have scarlet-red bark. *Salix daphnoides* (violet willow) has pewtery-purple young stems and pussy willows in spring. All you do is hack them back hard every year in February, and you get a new crop of long straight stems ready to use. I like hacking things back – you just chop them right down to about 6 inches from the ground. Lovely job.

Dogwood (*Cornus alba* 'Sibirica'). It's not only willow you can coppice for crafts. Dogwood is good too. It doesn't take up so much room, but it has bright red bark on the young stems too. Hack them back in February.

Hazel (*Corylus avellana*). The other good craft plant is hazel. This is what they use to make the rustic hurdles and twiggy trellis you can buy, but it's very easy to make your own. Cut a few thick stems and push them into the ground about 6 inches apart, then weave thinner stems round them. If you are making fencing it's easiest to make it up where it's going to stay. Hazel isn't such a pretty plant in the garden as dogwood and willow, but it is good for the wild garden and you can keep coppicing it for years – which also stops it getting too big. If there's anything over, just put it into your wood-burning stove.

Corkscrew hazel (*Corylus avellana* 'Contorta') ▸ The other plant I've used is corkscrew hazel – it has wildly twisty stems with lots of wibbly-wobbly bits that make fantastic plant supports. You don't need to do anything to them, just cut long stems off and push them in round a clump of any floppy plants. We have a big bush of corkscrew hazel at the water gardens, and when it grows over the path I just hack it back so there are always a few bits ready to use.

Birch (*Betula pendula*). You can be quite creative with birch twigs too. They grow in big bunches like masses of thin 'besom broom' twigs and they are so thin they can be twisted right round into a circle – just tie them so they stay put, then hang your twiggy wreath on the wall. You can also lay a birch 'wreath' down flat and use it as the base for a table decoration. You can push grasses, seed-pods and dried flowers on short stalks in between the twigs for support, and maybe put a candle in a dish in the centre.

Grape-vine. Grape-vine is very trendy. I use lots of it, because the plant on my patio needs pruning every year or it takes over. You can only cut grape-vines in winter and

early spring, or the stems bleed badly and you can kill the plant. Just chuck an armful of prunings into the shed and use them when you feel like it. Vine stems are great because they are so supple. I make the main structure of a fence panel or a bit of trellis out of hazel or willow poles, then weave bits of vine through them. Because it's so bendy, you can also wind vine stems into a tight knot, like a big ball of wool, and push it on to a pole as a rustic finial. You don't even need to fix it.

Garden prunings. If you can't find anything else, save up any long thin fruit tree prunings, though they don't bend very much. Bamboo stems, and ordinary garden canes, are good for making trellis or plant support frames but they are no good for anything that needs bending, as they just snap.

OTHER IDEAS

LIVING WILLOW STRUCTURES

An interesting new idea that is starting to get popular is to use fresh willow wands to make living willow structures. What makes them different from other kinds of 'twiggy crafts' is that the stems actually take root and grow, so your structure gradually blossoms into a live shape covered in green shoots.

To make them, you need long willow wands or withies for the bigger structures; if you don't have willows in your garden you can buy live withies from willow specialists by post. They sometimes advertise in gardening magazines. Prepare the ground just as if you were making a border – dig in some compost and fertilizer – then push the ends of the willow wands in about 6 inches or a foot, and keep them watered so they root and grow. To keep the shape, you need to clip back the shoots close to the main structure each spring. They look brilliant, and it's great fun to do.

* Living 'cage' round a container. This is really easy to do and looks great. Just take a dozen or so 4-foot live willow shoots, and strip all the leaves off except for a foot or so at the very top. Push them in round the side of a pot of flowers. Tie the tops together about 6 inches from the end, leaving a spray of foliage as a sort of flourish. The stems will take root so the leaves at the top stay fresh – looks like a very fashionable basket, but it takes about 2 minutes to make.
* Living screen. Push a row of long willow wands about 3 feet apart into soil that's been dug over, then bend the tops over and push them into the ground too, so you get a row of overlapping half-moon shapes.
* Arch or tunnel. Take two bundles of long withies, tied together at each end and in the middle so you have quite a thick support. Bend them over a path to make an arch, and tie them together at the top. If you want a tunnel, just make several arches a couple of feet apart along your path.

NATURAL DECORATION

I like to play around with little arty ideas for the garden just because it's fun, but if you are having friends round – or, better still, having a proper outdoor party with all the trimmings – then you really have an excuse for some serious decorating. You don't always want something big and stunning that will be the centre of attention. It's much nicer for people just to spot interesting little things dotted around, so long as they all follow the same sort of theme. A natural look, using things that you grow in the garden, would always be my first choice, but anything with a nice plant or garden feeling would be okay too. Little natural knick-knacks are a great way to dress up your patio or gazebo for dinner without making it look too over the top. I like things stuck in pots, too, as you can redecorate in minutes. There are loads of fun things that are quick to make, that look impressive, and that you can make up in advance. It gives you something creative to do in the long winter evenings when you are half-watching TV. You can start and finish a whole project at once, and you don't have to spend ages clearing up afterwards.

PLANTING BUNDLES OF WILLOW WITHY UPRIGHTS

A handful of stems are a good way to make instant garden art. You can use natural hazel, bought beanpoles or coloured willow wands. Curly hazel can look very good too.

1. **Take a handful of long straight bare willow stems, all about the same length, and bind them tightly together in a bundle.**
2. **Push them into the ground – you could plant something round them, but what looks really arty is to tuck them in between dense-packed plants in a border. Or you could shove a bundle into a pot of sand as an instant decoration on the patio, or even indoors.**

PLANTING BUNDLES OF WILLOW WITHY UPRIGHTS

NATURAL DECORATIONS

* Collage. Use an old wooden seed-tray as a 'frame' and fill it with slices of stuck-on cow parsley stems, poppy seed-heads or fir cones to make a natural collage to hang on the wall.
* Candlestick. Sit a short fat candle in a natural hollow in a big craggy chunk of driftwood to use as a giant candleholder. If you are using candles on your dinner table, the sort sold specially for flower arrangers are good as they melt very slowly, so they won't burn down and set fire to your table decoration before you finish eating.
* Plant holder. Hollow out the top of a big knotty tree stump and stand a pot of trailing plants such as nasturtiums in it so they trail artistically round the bumps – you can bung it in a corner of the patio and no one will know it hasn't been there for ages. It's also a good way to hide a manhole cover that just happens to be in the wrong place – they always are.

FLORAL ART

You can grow all sorts of things to make natural decorations with. Flowers and plants look lovely in the middle of tables or for putting round the patio or in your gazebo. Even just a few wildflowers in a jar can look great. The simpler the better.

* Floating flowers. I saw a very nice idea at a house recently where they had just floated a lot of flower-heads in a shallow bowl full of iced water. It looked brilliant, but it's very quick and easy to do.
* Hydrangea heads are great, as one flower makes a decoration on its own and you don't even need to stand it in water – you can poke the stem down the hole in the middle of a garden table that they leave for your sunshade to stand in – and the flower won't wilt, it just starts to dry out naturally.

BUTCHER'S BROOM

One plant I'm very keen on is butcher's broom. This is an odd thing that grows even in very deep shade: it's evergreen and has peculiar reptilian leaves like the scales of an armadillo. In the old days they really did use it as butcher's brooms – they used to tie bundles of stems together and use them for sweeping out the shop. I like to tie up little bundles of the leafy stems and hang them from the rafters of my pergola, if there's a bare-looking spot. And it's dead easy to truss a bunch of stems round the end of a thick bamboo cane with some hairy hessian string to make an instant homegrown patio broom – it looks really good leaning casually in a corner, even if you don't actually use it.

FOUND ART

If you are the sort of person who is always coming back from a walk with seashells, pine-cones, knotty bits of wood or handfuls of dried seaweed, use them to decorate the garden. With a bit of imagination they can look great.

* Collector's nightmare. You can make even quite small unrelated bits and pieces look artistic by piling them into a big glass jar. If you want to leave it out in the open, use something with a lid, like a giant spaghetti jar, so it doesn't fill up with water when it rains. After parties, collect up your old corks and use them in big jars.

HANGING OUT

Hanging baskets and wall planters need quite a bit of regular watering, but I've found a good way to get the effect without any of the work: cheat. Stuff the container with moss or make a 'nest' of birch twigs or fir cones – anything that will hold the stems in place – and then push dried hydrangea heads, seedpods and grasses in to make a sort of outdoor flower arrangement.

You can make up containers for a special occasion, but if you have a very sheltered patio or gazebo, or a wall that is protected from the weather by a bit of overhanging roof or a pergola, you should be able to leave them out all summer before they start to deteriorate. This is also quite a good way to make cheap outdoor Christmas decorations for the garden – you can always spray-paint the hydrangea heads and seedheads to give them a new look. Dead easy, and dead cheap, but it works well because it's not what most people expect to find in the garden.

WILD WATER

Everyone tells me how nice it must be to have a real river running through the garden. At work, the River Test runs round three sides of the garden centre so it's almost on an island. Further downstream, it goes right under my house, which was once the old mill cottage. A natural river looks great, and it makes the most amazing backdrop for plants, but you wouldn't believe how much work it makes.

In winter the banks get washed away, so every few years we have to reinforce them with sandbags. It takes ages, and as we can only do it in winter, we spend all our time thigh-deep in freezing cold water. The other thing we have to do is cut the water weed. Not on the banks – in the river itself. Water weed grows like mad, and when enough builds up it affects the flow of the water – and the river has to be properly managed because of all the trout fishing nearby. So we are given five or ten days in summer to cut the weeds. You just get in there and hack them back with a scythe. It must look crazy – like hay-making underwater. But at least all the neighbours with riverbanks on their property will be out doing the same thing at the same time. Then someone has to catch up the loose weed and yank it out afterwards, or it rots in the water and takes all the oxygen out of it, which is no good for the fish.

But you don't need a trout stream running through your garden to get a wild watery effect. If there's room for a pond, you'll get dragonflies swooping over it, frogs croaking, and lots of fabulous reflections – waterside plants like gunnera often look their best seen upside down. Even in a tiny space you could fit in a 'puddle' of water for frogs to breed in and birds and hedgehogs to drink out of – a few gnarled bits of log and some suitably wild-looking plants are all the extras you need.

MAKING A 'PUDDLE'

A wildlife pond is more like a big puddle than a normal garden pond. Instead of dropping straight down into relatively deep water, the sides are shallow and sloping so that wildlife can drink and bathe. A 'puddle' makes a little water-hole for wildlife, but it is also an easy alternative for anyone who is too busy to look after a fully stocked pond. When you've first made it, it'll be 2 or 3 years before you need to do anything at all. Then just dig up any overgrown perennial plants from round the edge in spring, divide them up, and replant one small piece in the same spot. If the pond fills up with water weed, remove handfuls in summer to thin it out. And if you get duckweed floating on the surface, skim it off with a net. Apart from that, leave it alone as much as possible. Dead easy. Natural-style ponds look really good edged with logs. You can make little planting pockets with them, to grow ferns in. Logs are very frog- and toad-friendly too – there are loads of damp holes underneath for the creatures to climb into in summer, and in winter they hibernate in the mud underneath.

1. It's not difficult to put a wildlife 'puddle' among mature plants in an existing semi-wild border, as I'm doing here. Clear the area of weeds and debris, and use the spade to roughly mark out an informal puddle-shape.
2. Dig it out, making the sides slope gently. Since this is just a puddle, and it's not going to have fish or water-lilies in it, a foot or so deep is just fine. Because the area is full of big tree roots which could easily pierce the pond liner, I'm lining the hole first with bonded fibre, which is like a tough, thick, fleecy underblanket.
3. Lay a sheet of pond liner over the hole, and let it drop down on top of the fibre lining. This is a good quality PVC liner, which is a lot cheaper than the usual butyl rubber kind.
4. Run a hosepipe into the pond so it starts to fill with water. Tweak the liner as the weight of water presses it down – you need to even out the worst folds so they make regular tucks all round.
5. Fill the pond to the top, then 'trim off' the surplus liner about a foot from the edge by burying it in the ground. Hide the edges of the liner with logs and bits of flat stone.

6. Plant a few overhanging plants round the edge – these are hardy ferns, which will be quite happy in light dappled shade.
7. Spread some small smooth stones all round the edges, tucking them underneath nearby plants.
8. By the time you've finished the edges are all hidden, and there are plants overhanging the water, so the pool looks exactly like a natural feature that has been there for ages.

MAKING A 'PUDDLE'

Unlike a normal pond where you sink water plants grown in pots into the water, here you only need to buy small strands of plants – or get bits from a friend with a pond when they are 'thinning out' surplus water plants in late spring – and just drop them in or plant them in the mud round the banks.

BOG GARDEN PLANTS: FOR MOIST BOGGY SOIL
ROUND THE EDGES OF A WILDLIFE 'PUDDLE'
Aruncus dioicus (goat's rue). Knee-high plants with ferny foliage and big frothy creamy white flower-heads in mid to late summer.
Rodgersia podophylla ▶ Big tall plants with late summer flowers and stunning foliage that looks good all season even when the plant's not in flower.
Hardy ferns. Wonderful textured foliage, good for light or dappled shade. There are loads of different kinds – the ones with frilly or lacy foliage are specially lovely.
Carex elata 'Aurea' (Bowles' golden sedge). Tussocks of loose grassy golden foliage, fabulous shapes in lemon and lime stripes.

WILDLIFE POND PLANTS: TO GROW IN THE WATER
Bog bean (Menyanthes trifoliata) has lovely foliage that runs out over the water, and pretty fringed white flowers in late spring and early summer. You don't need to plant a whole plant – you can buy strands that you just lay in the water and they root themselves into the banks.

OXYGENATORS
Plant a small piece in the middle of the pond to oxygenate the water and make a natural balance that keeps a pond healthy.
Myriophyllum is like lots of tiny Christmas trees poking up through the water, a great texture that contrasts nicely with plants round the edge of the pond.

WILDLIFE DITCH
If you don't have the sort of garden where a 'puddle' fits in, try a wildlife ditch – it looks nice and natural and it's really easy to make.
* First dig your ditch, about a foot deep. You can run it straight along the front of a hedge, like you find in farmland, or you can make it curved so it looks like a bit of dried-up stream bed running through grass and shrubs in a semi-wild garden. The great thing about a ditch is that even if it dries out in summer there's often a lot of

damp soil deeper down, so many moisture-loving waterside plants like kingcups and mimulus will grow there quite happily.

* To make sure the bottom stays damp I often make a bog garden in it. When I dig it out, I'll bury a sheet of polythene in the bottom, so it acts as a water reservoir – you only need to cover the very bottom of the ditch, it's not like lining a pond where you want the water level to come right up to the rim. With a ditch, you only want an inch or so of water in the bottom. Put enough soil over the polythene so you can't see it.

* The most natural way to landscape a ditch is to lay turf over the banks and run it down into the ditch – this looks great planted with ladies' smock and primroses, which are okay with the competition from grass. Or make a pebbly bank with just a few clumps of bigger damp-loving plants like water figwort and lythrum for a more structural effect.

GARDENING WITH WILDLIFE

I like to see lots of wildlife about the place. Hedgehogs are fun – at the water gardens, ours get the leftover catfood – and we get loads of bats whizzing about over the water after midges on summer evenings when the last customers have gone. But you don't have to have a totally wild garden to get lots of wild visitors. It's very easy to combine things that make a garden interesting for us with things that make wildlife feel at home – much better than watching them second-hand on TV.

If I did nothing else, I'd have a proper hedge. Hedges are much more wildlife-friendly than walls or fences. Mixed hedges are best. I like the rugged sort you see growing round fields out in the country, where you have a mixture of hazel, blackthorn and wild rose with an occasional elderberry or hawthorn tree growing up through the middle, or great tufts of vetches and bryony growing over the top. But you need the right sort of garden for that.

Otherwise, what you could do instead is plant a semi-wild hedge, which looks a bit more cultivated. Use a mixture of shrubs like species roses, the kind with lots of hips, a few buddleias, and one or two of the ornamental elders – there are several very pretty kinds with coloured or variegated foliage as well as fruit. If you are worried about birds eating the elderberries and leaving purple blobs all over your car or your washing, then just hack them hard back every couple of years so they don't get any fruit – the foliage just grows better instead, and the birds still find plenty of less messy stuff to eat.

Even that is probably not on for your smart executive housing estate. What I'd do there is plant a more formal hedge that needs clipping only twice a year, and leave it thick enough so that birds can get right inside to nest in it. I love green and purple beech planted alternately. The colours grow together, making a swirly pattern that always reminds me of the marble cake I used to love making as a kid. If marble cake hedges don't hold the same fond memories for you, or you don't have enough room, you can get a pretty passable alternative by putting up fences and growing lots of ivies over them. Once they make a good thick covering, they are amazing wildlife sanctuaries full of nesting pockets, insects, beetles and all sorts.

PLANTING A WILDLIFE HEDGE

A wildlife hedge makes a nice natural boundary for a wild area, and can be very colourful. The idea is to use a mixture of different shrubs, chosen because they provide food for birds, butterflies and bees as well as colourful flowers and foliage, and to plant them quite close together in a line. Here, I've used buddleia, *Viburnum opulus*, sea buckthorn (*Hippophäe rhamnoides*) and *Physocarpus* 'Dart's Gold'. Lots of people like to plant a hedge in autumn or spring, but when you are using pot-grown plants like these you can do it any time of year unless the soil is too wet or cold to dig.

1. After marking out a strip about 18 inches wide running the whole length of the place you want to put your hedge, and digging out the weeds, beginning at one end, scoop out a planting hole a bit bigger than the pots your plants are growing in.
2. Put a good helping of well-rotted compost, manure or tree-planting compost into the bottom of the planting hole and stir it round with a fork. Then spread some more on the soil you'll use to fill the hole in with, and mix well.

3. Lift your first plant out of its pot – bang the bottom down hard on a brick to loosen it, if it doesn't come out easily. There's no need to break up the rootball, but if it is packed really tight then I'd just tease out a few coils from the bottom to encourage them to grow out into the soil. Now stand the plant in the hole, check that the top of the rootball is level with the surrounding soil, and use your soil mixture to fill what's left of the hole. Firm the soil gently round the roots.
4. I find it easiest to arrange the plants in a row along the edge of my prepared planting strip first. That way I can make sure I don't have two of the same kind together, and that neighbouring plants look okay next to each other. I've stood them 18 inches apart here, which is the right spacing for a wildlife hedge.

5. Water the plants in well, and keep them watered in dry weather until they are established. There's no regular clipping or trimming to do with this type of hedge – just leave the shrubs to grow into each other and only prune out the odd branch if it spoils the shape. Feed by sprinkling Growmore along the soil both sides of the row every spring.

6. As soon as it's all planted, the hedge looks like it really belongs there. I've left the old fence-posts as they add a bit of atmosphere, but you could run 2 or 3 strands of wire along them to define your boundary until the plants fill the space.

5

PLANTING A WILDLIFE HEDGE

6

CARING FOR A WILDLIFE HEDGE

* Keep the plants watered in dry weather until they are growing well on their own (you won't usually need to water again if you plant them in autumn, as nature does it for you.
* There's no need to cut a hedge like this – just let the shrubs grow into each other, and if necessary cut back any shoots that are too long or grow out in funny places and spoil the shape of the hedge. It's supposed to look more like a row of shrubs, not a formal clipped hedge.
* Feed the hedge each spring by sprinkling a handful per metre of a general fertilizer such as blood, fish and bone along the soil each side of it.

WAYS TO ATTRACT WILDLIFE

Wildlife don't just lounge around the place eating berries and fruit and splashing about in your pool. A lot of the time they feed on things that gardeners are keen to get rid of, so anything you do to encourage them really pays off. Hedgehogs, for instance, eat slugs and snails, birds take all kinds of grubs and caterpillars, and there are also a whole lot of predatory insects such as hoverflies and ladybirds with a taste for greenfly. Even wasps clear up lots of garden pests, until the plum season starts and they think of better things to do. One of the things I really love about wandering round the garden is finding something to pick and nibble as I go, like wild strawberries or blackberries. Wildlife do too. But anything edible or useful you grow is going to bring more wildlife into the garden. There are three things that really make a garden friendly for wildlife – shelter, food and water. Include a bit of each to attract more wildlife into your patch.

* Safe places. A few big trees and shrubs with ground-cover plants like periwinkle growing under them are perfect for creating shelter. Birds can sit in there, keeping a look-out for cats and other predators. You can make your trees even more attractive by hanging up bird feeders or balls of fat in them in winter. And if you have a big tree, you could nail up a couple of nestboxes – all the fun of parenthood without the responsibility.
* Mess. Wildlife don't like a garden that is always being disturbed, so it's no good being too neat and tidy. They like plenty of hidey-holes, so leave piles of rotting logs and dead leaves or even lawn mowings lying around – I know a chap who has a hatching of grass snakes in his compost heap every year – or you can half-bury a wooden box for hedgehogs to hibernate in. There's nothing like a bit of rotting vegetation to attract insects and beetles, which just about everybody eats.
* Seed-heads. Decorative grasses with big fat seed-heads are good, and so are things like allium seed-heads, so don't bother dead-heading them. One thing that always attracts loads of finches is bronze fennel; and leave a patch of groundsel or wild thistles down the garden – they love them too.

* Fruit and berries. All sorts of things like windfall apples, blackberries and ornamental crab-apples attract wildlife, but you should grow shrubs with loads of berries like cotoneaster and pyracantha, *Rosa rugosa* and amelanchier too.
* Artificial inducements. Put out pet fur combings at nesting times, peanuts, fat and bird-seed in winter, leftover catfood any time of year for birds and hedgehogs, and whole overripe fruit but not just peel or cores.
* Water. Make sure there's always water to drink – a small pond is good but you can just sink a big old meat dish into the ground, fill it with water and put a few pebbles in the bottom so birds have something to wrap their toes round.
* Nectar-rich plants. Organic gardeners have got the knack of attracting helpful insects by planting the right sort of flowers. You often see rows of nectar plants like *Phacelia tanacetifolia*, *Limnanthes douglasii* (poached egg plant), buckwheat and calendula marigold growing down the bottom of an organic garden, or in the vegetable bed, but they are good to put in your cottage garden too.
* Companion planting. The other great organic gardening tip is companion planting. The idea behind this is that certain plants give off natural chemicals that somehow protect their neighbours, and I've no idea if it works or not but you never know – anything is worth a try. You hear of people planting garlic with roses to ward off greenfly, and growing onions with carrots so the smell keeps off carrot fly. When I was doing a spot of pruning at a vineyard in New Zealand, they'd grow a little patch of rosemary and roses at the end of each row of vines. When I asked why, they said it was a traditional remedy for greenfly. I found it hard to believe, but as I never actually saw any aphids perhaps it does work – unless they were also spraying pesticides on the quiet.
* Moles. Wildlife isn't always a good thing for the garden. Personally, I like moles, though most gardeners don't. We had one in the kitchen at work once. I went in to make the coffee and there was a scraping noise which I thought was a mouse; but then out from under the washing-machine came a mole. Being an old house, the 'solid' floor can't be that thick so he must have dug up through a weak spot. He was very cute, 'swimming' out across the floor with that funny breast-stroke action moles use for tunnelling. I put him out in the garden and he burrowed out of sight in seconds. He's still there. We've got the molehills to prove it. There's no really effective way of stopping them – you hear of people putting musical birthday cards down the holes, or sticking milk-bottles into molehills so the wind blowing over the top makes funny noises underground. Personally I'd just put up with them. If you do manage to evict your resident mole, another one will only move into the vacant territory so you're no better off.

WALK-IN TREE-HOUSE

There's nothing like having a secret place; somewhere you can sit and read when you just want a bit of time to yourself. A tree-house is the hermit's choice – a cool, leafy 'den' where you can slump on some nice squashy cushions and nobody knows you are 'at home' if you keep quiet. But a proper tree-house takes time. You should have started about a hundred years ago! Unless you inherited a big mature tree with spreading branches ready to build in, you'll have to convert your own ground-level Des Res. It doesn't cost a bomb, you won't spill your tea getting in there, and you can move in straight away.

At the water gardens, in one of the wilder bits, we've got a big weeping birch with branches that trail right down to the ground. We've cut a gap in one side so you can get under the canopy, and children love it in there. Someone put a sculpture of a fawn inside – it's lying in the long grass – and I'm always finding kids in there stroking it and talking to it.

If you've already got a good-sized weeping tree, it's easy enough just to take out a couple of branches and maybe put in a pair of curvy bean-poles tied at the top to make a rustic arch to go in through. All you need is a log or a small bench underneath to sit on, and a fat wooden log standing on end to use as a table. Since it's too dark under most weeping trees for grass to grow, you need to put something down on the ground to make it a bit cosier – the easy way is just to tip out a couple of bags of bark or granite

chippings and rake them around. For more of a tree-house effect you could make a log floor. If you don't happen to have a suitable tree in the garden already, just plant a new weeping tree and it won't be long before the branches grow to make a curtain that gives you your tree-house shape.

Autumn is the very best time to plant a tree – the soil is still warm but the weather is rainy, so the roots can really get stuck in. But if you don't mind keeping it watered in dry weather, you can plant any time you like, even in summer.

1. When you are planting a tree in the lawn, remove the turf from a circle about 4 feet across. Skim it off with a spade to a depth of about 1½ inches – that way you get rid of the roots too, so you won't have a weed problem later.

2. Fork the ground over to loosen it up. If you find any big stones or roots, now's the time to take them out.

3. Dig the planting hole. Before putting the tree in, hammer a short stake in at an angle of about 45 degrees. The reason for doing this first is that you don't want to drive the stake through the tree's roots.

4. Tip plenty of tree-planting compost down the hole and mix it into the soil with a fork.

5. Stand the tree in the hole, and check that the top of the rootball is level with the surrounding soil. Mix some more tree-planting compost with the soil you took out of the hole, shovel it back round the roots, and firm gently. Then use a proper tree tie to secure the tree to the stake – not the stake to the tree (as they always say at horticultural college!). Years ago they used long stakes for trees and they just fell over as soon as the stake rotted, but now the idea is to tie trees low down, leaving the top free to bend in the wind, so the tree 'learns' to grow a decent root system.

6. The weeping purple osier (*Salix purpurea* 'Pendula') is a lovely tree to plant near water, but unlike the usual weeping willow it won't grow too big or be a nuisance in a smaller garden. It'll be a couple of years before you can sit under this one.

PLANTING A TREE

RUSTIC PAVILIONS

If you want more headroom, or just a bigger floor area under your weeping tree, train it into a circular 'pavilion'.

* Use rustic poles radiating out like the spokes of a wheel to make the roof, supported on some nice craggy uprights.
* Plant a weeping tree in the middle. Choose one with a good shape, with a tall straight trunk so the branches start high enough for you to get in underneath. It doesn't matter if the crown of the tree isn't quite as high as the 'roof', as you can lift the branches up on to it – they'll just make a funnel shape in the middle which can look quite nice and crypt-like.
* Spread the branches out and tie them over the 'bones' of the structure.
* Add your own extras, like a circular tree seat round the trunk.

SECRET PLACES FOR ANY GARDEN

* If you wanted a faster result, you could put trellis over the top and sides of your pavilion and grow big climbers over it – wisteria or a grape-vine would be very nice.
* Ivies take a bit longer to get going, but once the stems covered the top and started to weave into each other, you would have an evergreen tree-house that would look brilliant in winter and be nice and cool in summer.
* You don't have to make a round tree-house either. If you have two walls making a right angle in a quiet corner of the garden, use rafters to make a quarter-circular pavilion between them.

SUITABLE TREES

For a walk-in tree-house, choose a well-shaped tree with lots of branches radiating out from the top at a suitable height. When it grows bigger, after a few years, don't be afraid

to hack out entire branches to stop the tree turning into a sort of 'Beatle wig' if you want a lighter effect. If you go for a pavilion, you'll need to train the tree over the wooden shape by cutting out branches that grow in the wrong place, and tying the rest to the timbers to hold them in place.

Purple weeping willow (*Salix purpurea* 'Pendula') ◄
The normal weeping willow gets far too big, too fast, and has damaging roots – this variety is well-behaved, with lovely purple stems. As you can see, it's also bendy enough to squeeze into the car!

Weeping birch (*Betula pendula* 'Youngii'). This has a lovely twiggy shape that looks like an upside-down nest in winter. It makes a good free-standing tree-house.

Persian ironwood (*Parrotia persica*). Gets quite big in time unless trained over a structure and pruned hard, like the ones at Castle Drogo in Devon. Incredible red and orange autumn leaves.

Weeping pear (*Pyrus salicifolia* 'Pendula') makes an elegant grey-leaved mound shape.

Weeping Siberian pea tree (*Caragana arborescens* 'Pendula'). An unusual tree with yellow pea flowers, good for small or windy gardens – it doesn't make a dense screen of foliage but it's good for training over a structure.

TOP TIP

LAYING A LOG FLOOR

Get a couple of bags of logs – the short, round, unsplit sort that they sell for firewood, or the sort joined together with packing tape as log-rolls for edging borders, sold at garden centres. Dig out the area for the floor about 8 inches deep, and set the logs on end. Pack gravel between them to hold them firmly in place so they won't wobble themselves loose when you walk on them. Or cover the area in a couple of inches of gravel and bed slices of log down into it, pushing them up close together to make a log 'pavement'. Use a mixture of sizes from big to little, so there are no big gaps in it. You can sometimes buy large log slices (people often use them for 'stepping stones' in a woodland garden), but if you are having a tree taken down, get the tree firm to slice a few bits off for you with the chainsaw.

OTHER IDEAS

PERGOLA-PLUS

I'm a great pergola fan. A pergola is a formal 'walk' with an open 'roof' of rafters held up by posts, all grown over with climbers. In my garden at home, I've turned one end of my pergola into an all-weather retreat by putting clear plastic over the top. You can't see it at all, as it's completely hidden by climbers that grow, hanging on to the trelliswork, underneath. But it keeps the rain off, so I can sit out there at any time of year. I'll often sit out there on my days off in early spring, wrapped in a blanket, with the radio. I love it. It's nice and cosy, you are out of the wind and rain, and you don't get sunburn. Very relaxing. And best of all, it's no big effort.

In America, you sometimes see stunning conifer canopies, which they make from a pergola with an unusual sprawly weeping blue cedar (*Cedrus atlantica* 'Glauca Pendula') trained out over the roof. This is a slow-growing conifer, and not very strong, so it needs training over a structure. It looks amazing when it's grown enough to cover the structure – just sheer curtains of blue needles draped down all round like some kind of exotic tent.

WET, WET, WET

Because my roots are in water gardening, the first things I want to see when I go to places like the Chelsea Flower Show are the water features. You get loads of them there – water is always a huge attraction. What makes Chelsea so special is the way garden designers fall over themselves to come up with new ideas every time. One year it's all natural rock pools you'd love to paddle in, the next it might be stainless steel with water running down mirrors, or there'll be a great big formal canal surrounded by giant date palms, freshly flown in from Arabia. The more outrageous the better!

That sort of thing's fine for a show like Chelsea, because it's *the* shop-window for the trade, but those really over-the-top water features are not terribly practical for your garden at home. For a start they cost an absolute fortune. The maintenance alone would be a nightmare. And if you have kids, you'd never dare let them out in the garden with so much slippery stone or open water around – you'd almost need your own lifeguard for some of them. (Now there's a hunky gardening tip.)

Small, safe, easily cared-for water features are what you want. There are loads of inspired but affordable ideas that are easy to do yourself. But you don't need real water at all. You can cheat. You can make it look like you had water yesterday, but it's not there today. Or you can have features that give the illusion of water where there isn't any – like your own private mirage. And you can have brilliant mini water features – even table-top ones – where there's so little water in them, you'd hardly believe your eyes. So don't be put off by the idea of real water, if it isn't practical for you. Just fake it.

DRY STREAMS

If you want a natural-style water feature that looks the part all year round, but doesn't have any actual water to worry about, there's one way to have it – cheat. Dig your own dry stream bed and decorate it with all the things that go with real wild water – rocks, wildflowers or dry-land versions of waterside plants. There are plenty of naturally occurring variations on the stream theme that you can draw your inspiration from, so there's something to suit every style of garden. A dry stream is lots less work and far cheaper to make than the real thing – besides being totally safe where small children are likely to be running around.

DESIGNING AND MAKING A DRY STREAM BED

The one thing all natural stream beds have in common is they never run in a straight line. Even winterbournes, which often run along the end of a garden or the edge of a field, will be wider in some places than others and have alternate deep and shallow patches, which makes a more irregular outline. I'm not one of those paper and pencil planners, so the way I go about designing a feature like this is on the spot. Then you can plant it straight away.

1. **Use a bit of hosepipe to roughly mark out the shape. A gently winding shape looks best. It needs to be about 2 feet wide to look reasonably realistic. Before making your mind up where the hosepipe 'stream' looks best, get a bird's-eye view out of an upstairs window and also see what it looks like from other angles – the kitchen window, the garden gate, the patio and any of the places you normally sit or look out over the garden. It's still very quick and easy to make any adjustments at this stage. Once you know where your stream is to go, start digging. Just make a ditch – it doesn't need to be very deep – even 6 inches is enough to create the illusion. To make it look natural, give it a rounded bottom so it looks as if it was carved by running water. You can throw the soil up along each edge to make sloping banks, but if you are running your stream through a border as I am here, I'd just spread the soil out over the beds to keep it looking more level.**

2. When the digging is done, go over the area carefully and pick out any weeds, especially roots of perennial weeds like nettles – you don't want them coming up through your pebbles later.
3. You can adapt the basic stream shape to suit almost any style of garden. It just depends how you landscape it. A very minimalist dry stream with just a few well-placed chunks of rock and grasses looks really amazing.
4. Spread 1 to 2 inches of gravel all over the stream bed, remembering to firm and flatten the soil down beforehand to prevent it quickly sinking in, then tip out a couple of bags of smooth pebbles to add extra character to key places. In nature, the bigger bits of stones end up along the deepest bit of the stream, so that's the way to use them here if you want a fairly realistic result.

DESIGNING AND MAKING A DRY STREAM BED

CHECK THE POSITIONING

Don't just dig out a feature like this 'by eye' and hope it looks right – the odds are it won't, and it'll take ages to alter later. Get it right from the start. The easy way to do this is to mark out several different alternative shapes using the hosepipe method. Stand your 'key' plants roughly in place – still in their pots – plus maybe a few big cobbles, so you can get a good idea what it really looks like, then take a Polaroid snap. When you've got snaps of three or four different potential schemes lined up, it's easy to compare them and pick the one you like best to go ahead with, *before* you start on the heavy work. Saves ages!

* Pebbly or drought gardens. On Mediterranean hillsides, at the end of a hot summer, they get really heavy storms that send flash floods through deeply etched channels in the ground. You can adapt this look for the garden by using a range of different coloured sands going down to the bottom of the stream bed, where you use finer sand. I wouldn't use too many pebbles in the actual bed of the stream – it looks better with just a few big bits of stone and rock and some tufts of grassy-looking plants growing up between them. Festucas are perfect for dry soil; some of the small sedges that suit normal garden soil rather than really boggy conditions are good here too, such as *Acorus gramineus* 'Ogon', which has green and cream striped fans of foliage, or *Carex comans*, which has fine reddish brown leaves.
* Natural style or country gardens. The English countryside is full of winding streams that slow to a trickle in summer. At home in Hampshire we have winterbournes – dry stream beds that sit there all summer and then suddenly start flowing one day in winter when there's been enough rain up in the hills. You could make a stream bed in a lawn with turf running down the banks, a few clumps of wild flowers, and

just swirls of pebbles and damp-lovers like hostas, hardy ferns and corkscrew rush growing in the bottom. What looks nice with this is a bridge. It could be something very simple like a couple of railway sleepers, or you could lay a fallen log across and maybe train a climber like a honeysuckle over it. I rather like the idea of putting a couple of trolls or a stone rabbit half hidden under the bridge, so when you are standing on it there is a 'surprise' to look out for. Or else put in some flat stepping-stones in a line across a wider part of the stream bed.

MAKING A STREAM OF BULBS

Without doing any digging at all, you can use plants to create the illusion of natural water. Just use plants whose colours or shapes look like water, and grow them in the shape of a stream. Okay, they won't fool anyone for long – though seen from a distance your first impression can be surprisingly realistic – but they do make very attractive, unusual and totally safe 'water' features that add loads of character to a garden.

If you like to bring new ideas regularly into the garden, or you just don't want to commit yourself to a long-lasting feature, then I'd use short blue-flowered annuals for making a summer stream. In a more contemporary sort of garden, you can go for blue grasses 'running' through gravel. But in a fairly natural-style garden, short blue flowers make quite a realistic-looking stream winding their way through trees or shrubs. You can use spring bulbs for creating this effect, as they are there one season and gone the next – it's just what happens in nature when real streams dry up in summer.

This looks great under trees or in a big border running through shrubs, and it looks wonderful in spring when the bulbs are all out in flower. To give a reasonable suggestion of running water, you've really got to pack the bulbs in when you are planting – you don't want too much bare soil.

1. Fork the ground over, remove any weeds and rubbish, and rake it roughly level.
2. Use hosepipe to help you plan out the scheme. Mark out a naturally flowing shape, which can vary in width as it runs round shrubs or other features. The good thing about using hosepipe is that it's very easy to keep changing your mind until you come up with a shape you like.
3. Spread the bulbs out over the ground a few inches apart. The way to get a really natural look is to drop them from about waist height and plant them where they fall – that way, you won't end up with straight lines.
4. Use a trowel or proper bulb planter to put them in – just make a hole the right depth, drop the bulb down it, then fill the hole. Use your imagination a little to picture the final result, but look at the picture of the grape hyacinth on page 142 for a better idea.

MAKING A STREAM OF BULBS

PLANTING AND GROWING BULBS

* Dry, dormant spring bulbs are sold in garden centres in late summer and autumn. You can also buy them from bulb catalogues – the ones selling spring bulbs come out in summer so you can order in time for autumn delivery.
* Spring bulbs need to be planted as soon as possible after you get them. Don't keep them hanging about till they dry out and shrivel. They need plenty of time in the ground to grow roots and get their act together before they start flowering.
* Bulbs need to be planted deeper than you think – make a hole four times as deep as the bulbs are, measured from tip to toe, and drop them into the bottom of it pointed end up.
* Once they've been planted, you don't need to do anything except feed bulbs once a year – water them with diluted tomato feed when they are in bud, or just as the flowers go over.
* Don't be in too much hurry to tidy up the foliage after bulbs have finished flowering – the plants need it to swell the bulbs up ready for next year. Wait 6 weeks before cutting off the leaves or, if they are growing in grass, before mowing that bit of the lawn.

PLANTS FOR A FLOWER STREAM

Plant your bulbs or flowers quite close together to give a really dense effect. It's far better only to make a small feature with lots of impact, than a bigger one that looks rather half-hearted.

Bluebells look very natural planted as a stream in shade under trees or in wild woodland. Don't try to get wild English bluebells, use the bigger Spanish bluebells which you can buy easily as dry bulbs. Only use bluebells where you don't mind them spreading, because they will. A natural setting is best as the foliage looks a bit messy for a long time after they finish flowering, which makes them unpopular with very tidy gardeners. Plant them about 6 inches apart and 4 inches deep.

Blue annual flowers look good for a temporary summer stream. Any kinds that grow 6 inches high or less could be used, if they have masses of flowers and a long flowering season. You could use all the same kind, or be a bit arty and use several different shades of blue dotted together with a few white or silver-foliage plants to make more of a sun-on-the-water sparkling effect. Good flowers to use are blue shades of viola, lobelia, and anagallis. Watch out if you are relying on descriptions in catalogues or on plant labels, as a lot of flowers the writers call 'blue' are actually shades of purple, which doesn't look half so realistic planted as a stream. Try to see the plants in flower before buying them, to be sure they are true blue.

Grape hyacinths ▼ have a really intense blue. Plant the bulbs about 2 inches apart and 3 inches deep. Blue festuca grasses are good for a contemporary-style stream in a patch of gravel or as a small 'pool' in a dry garden; plant the clumps 6 to 9 inches apart.

FAKE WATER FEATURE

A bog garden, planted with natural moisture-lovers, is the very best way I know to turn a problem wet bit of garden with awful clay soil into a really glamorous garden feature. The thing I love about bog plants is they are so lush and green, and so many of them have really dramatic foliage, which makes a bog garden look good even if there isn't much out in flower. But then, I'm biased – bog garden perennials are some of my very favourite plants of all. If you can't have real water in the garden, a bog garden is the next best thing. Even in a tiny garden, you can always go for a bog garden in a pot. You could just have one big plant like a gunnera in a trendy pot with the leaves partly 'mirrored' by a shallow tray of water, or mix several bog plants together in a matching container – there are some lovely ceramic ones around. It can look stunning, and it's so quick and easy to do.

MAKING A BOG IN A POT

Choose a large container – for a potted bog garden it doesn't need to have any drainage holes in the bottom, but if yours does have holes, choose a matching tray to stand it in so it can hold lots of water. You'll need a selection of shorter clumpier plants suitable for growing in moist to boggy soil, but nothing that grows too tall or it'll outgrow the arrangement. Bowles' golden sedge, creeping Jenny and hostas or a really damp-loving fern would be brilliant. Tidy them up first by taking off any dodgy-looking leaves.

1. **Part fill the container with compost. At the water garden we make up our own, specially to grow bog plants in, but at home any good brand of potting compost is fine.**
2. **Start planting. It's just like using bedding plants – take them out of their pots and stand them in place. Put the tallest plants like this holly fern towards the back, so they make a background for shorter plants and give you a more 'arranged' look.**
3. **Pack the plants close together – this is one place where an overcrowded look works best. Something trailing over the front looks good. This is the golden form of creeping Jenny. Finish off by sprinkling some small stones between the plants to cover the compost. It looks good, and also stops the moisture evaporating too fast.**
4. **Give the container a really generous watering – you want the water to soak the compost, and fill the tray at the bottom too.**

MAKING A BOG IN A POT

CARING FOR A BOG IN A POT

* Keep the water level well topped up. These are plants that aren't going to like drying out one little bit, but if they are up to their necks in water they'll be perfectly happy. If you use a pot without drainage holes, you can just fill it up to the rim every few days.

* In winter, when bog plants are dormant, they don't need to be quite so wet but if the pot fills up with water they won't mind either.

* In spring, it's best to tip the tub out and start again with fresh potting compost. Divide up any plants that have grown too big and just re-pot one piece of each – the rest you can plant in the garden.

* In summer, keep them good and wet. Cut off dead flower-heads as it keeps the container looking tidy, and it helps keep the foliage in good condition for longer.

ALTERNATIVE POTTED BOG GARDEN

A good way to cheat at bog gardening is to make a bog in a tray. Buy several small damp-loving plants in pots. Instead of planting them into a bigger container, leave them in their pots. If they are bursting out of their garden-centre pots, or the original pots look a bit naff, re-pot them into clay pots one size bigger than the old ones. Then just stand them in a big shallow tray of water. To look after them, all you do is top the tray up every few days so they are always standing in an inch or two of water.

There are several compact kinds of damp-loving sedges and grassy plants that look good in pots, and hostas are specially brilliant – they are nice and compact, and not so top-heavy that they're always toppling over. And the foliage is amazing – you get blues, greens, gold, curly, variegated and stripy leaves. Apart from looking good, the other benefit from growing hostas this way is that there's less hassle with slugs. It's like growing them in their own castle, surrounded by a moat – and slugs can't swim. Yet!

TRICKS WITH SHALLOW WATER

If you have a tray of shallow water with plants standing in it, put a few drops of food colouring into the water to liven it up. Use the sort sold for cake icing – cake-craft shops sell all sorts of colours you can't get in the supermarket, but even the usual green, blue or violet can look great. You only need a hint of colour.

Or get some black vegetable dye – you could just use ink – and put quite a lot into a very plain wide shallow bowl of water, so you can't see through the water. This makes a shallow pool look deeper, and much more mysterious. It makes a wonderful water feature surrounded by hardy ferns, hostas or bog plants. The reflections are really brilliant – it's a trick the landscapers use in their pools at big garden shows.

BIGGER BOG GARDENS

Bog gardens are brilliant, as they make it easy to grow all the bigger moisture-loving perennials in a really natural setting. To make a bog garden, dig out a hole about 2 feet deep and as wide as you like, then line the bottom 12 to 18 inches of it with a sheet of unperforated polythene. Fill the hole back up with a nice boggy mixture of garden soil and manure or compost, so it's level with the surrounding garden. Then just fill it with plants, anything that likes to live in damp soil – there are heaps of them. Even if you don't have a lot of room, you can make a bog garden look really lush. I'm not a person for spreading bog plants out and leaving them lots of room to grow. Jam 'em in there!

Maintenance is very easy. Just weed through in spring, then spread a couple of inches of thoroughly rotted garden compost or manure all over the soil. Plants love it. It helps keep the weeds down and the moisture in. Decorate with a few attractive bits of stone or a fallen log.

BOG PLANTS

Bowles' golden sedge (*Carex elata* 'Aurea') ◄ Long golden leaves which are brightest when it's grown in plenty of sun. Dies down in winter.

Creeping Jenny (*Lysimachia nummularia* 'Aurea'). Looks like strings of those gold-foil-covered chocolate coins you used to get at Christmas, but all strung together. And it has little yellow flowers in summer; looks lovely with Bowles' golden sedge.

Holly fern (*Cyrtomium falcatum*). An evergreen fern which is a real damp-lover, with very bold foliage.

Weeping sedge (*Carex pendula*). A 3-foot-high plant with really long dangly green 'tails' that remind you of cascading water. Although it's a bit tall, it's a good plant for a tub.

***Carex hachijoensis* 'Evergold'.** A short green and gold striped evergreen sedge with curving leaves instead of the very stiff ones some sedges have.

***Iris laevigata* 'Variegata'.** A water iris with variegated leaves, this looks good all summer instead of just when it's flowering – all the irises have a very short flowering season. It's one of my favourite plants. You'll find it with me on my desert island. A bog garden would be my one luxury.

TIDYING GRASSES AND OTHER GRASSY-LOOKING PLANTS

Grasses and grassy-looking plants are great for planting round all sorts of water gardens – real or fake. There are varieties suitable for dry, moist or really wet conditions and they all go brilliantly with pebbles and gravel. The perennial kinds that I use this way last for years, and though they are very simple to look after there's one thing you must do with them, and that is tidy them up occasionally – anything from a tease-out to a total haircut.

* Deciduous kinds naturally die down each year for the winter, and need hacking back hard to tidy them up in autumn. Cut the leaves off at ground level as soon as the plant looks like it is starting to die off.

* Evergreen grasses in theory keep their leaves all year round, but the oldest leaves often go a bit brown if there's a hard winter or a long dry spell in summer. If they don't look too bad you can just snip out the worst bits straight away. The very best time to do a major chop is the spring, when grasses are just starting to grow, as this way they soon replace the missing leaves. But you can usually get away with it at other times of year if you need to.

* Grasses with stunning seed-heads don't want cutting back until early spring, as besides feeding birds, the dead seed-heads look brilliant outlined with frost in midwinter. And with some grasses that turn brown in winter, like miscanthus, the brown foliage is part of the attraction. It gives lots of shelter and makes nice whispering noises, so just leave it.

REAL WATER

I love fountains. There's nothing like moving water to bring the garden to life – and it's so relaxing to sit and watch, whether you've got just a simple jet of water, a cherub tinkling in your lily pond, or a miniature Versailles. You can put fountains in shady places where water plants and fish would not be happy, to add a real sparkle to dark corners. They team up perfectly with hostas and hardy ferns. People always think you need a pond to have a fountain, but you don't. You can have water gushing up out of a pool of pebbles down the garden, or a rippling bowl of water on a patio table. And you don't have to buy expensive ready-made fountain features – in fact it's even more fun to try making your own. They can be much more creative and cheaper than the ones you buy, and it gives you a great excuse to play with water on a sunny day – just like being an overgrown kid.

If you've just won the lottery and are wondering how to spend your £2.8 million, you could start by ordering yourself a really brilliant water garden. Some of the stuff you can get now is out of this world. You can always tell the really outrageous gear – the words 'price on application' in the adverts are the clue. How about a water maze, like the one at Hever Castle in Kent? This is enormous fun. It's like a big pond with stepping stones so you can walk across it, except that some of the stepping stones are trick ones that squirt a jet of water straight up at you when you step on them. Kids love it, but lots of big kids are always out on it too. I had a great time, I got drenched.

Or you could have a remote-controlled fountain with built-in strobe lights that move to music. Then there are all sorts of Disneyland special effects like revolving fountains and jumping jets of water – I'm fascinated by the fountains with underwater lights that seem to flow with the water. None of these are the sort of thing you could put in for yourself unless you'd had an awful lot of experience creating water features, but frankly if you'd just won the lottery, you wouldn't care. You'd just call an expert in to do it for you.

Okay, day-dream over. The good news is you don't have to spend a fortune to have a very attractive contemporary-style water feature. What you want is a pebble pool: they look stunning but they're really easy to do. They are just the thing for a stylish modern look, surrounded by a sea of smooth pebbles decorated with clumps of grasses. And unlike a pond, there is virtually nothing to do once they are in place except sit and look at them – which is very relaxing. I could sit and watch water for hours.

With a pebble pool like this, there's no messing about – you just buy a semi-rigid shape, a drilled rock and a low-voltage pond pump. One that pumps 200 to 250 gallons of water per hour is quite powerful enough, because you only want a ripple of water, not a huge great jet. The great thing about pebble pools is that they are perfectly safe for children, as there isn't any standing water – it's all kept safely underground in a covered reservoir. But you still get birds dropping in for a drink or a shower. Preformed pebble pool bases come in several sizes, and they consist of two parts: a reservoir, and the perforated lid that fits over the top.

1. Dig out a hole big enough to sink the preformed pebble pool base up to its rim; make the hole the same shape as the reservoir with about an inch of free space all round.

2. Smooth damp sand all over the bottom of the hole to line it and act as a cushion for the plastic base, so sharp stones in the soil can't puncture it. Use soft building sand.

3. Fit the pebble pool reservoir into the hole. Sit the lid on, and lay a spirit level over the top to check that it's perfectly level – if it isn't, remove the pebble pool base and put a little extra sand in the hole to level it. Refit the base and lid, and check again until it's right.

4. Get some potting compost – much better than garden soil because there aren't any stones in it, and better than using sand round the sides because it's easier for plants to root into.

5. Use this to fill the gap between the pebble pool and the edge of the hole. Pack it well in so there's a really tight fit.

6. Now for the electrics. You want a bit of hosepipe long enough to reach from your water feature to the house. We're going to run the cable for your pump through this, so you don't damage it when you are hoeing or digging the garden. Tie a bit of string to a long nail and drop it down one end of the hose, then work it through to the far end.

7. When you reach the other end, untie the nail and tie the string to the end of the electric cable. Now you can draw the cable through the pipe. To connect your

pump up to a power supply, you need to drill through the wall near a handy socket, run the end of the cable through the wall and connect a 3-pin plug the other side. Plug it in via a circuit-breaker; you'll need room for a small transformer too, so don't choose a place where it's going to be too visible.

8. Place the submersible pump in the base of your pebble pool. There's a little groove in the plastic to lay the cable in so when you put the 'lid' on it sits level.

9. Now fit the bit of tubing provided to the water outlet from the pump. Most pumps come with several fountain jets, but for a feature like this you don't need one as you just want a low ripple of water. Fill the reservoir with water.

10. Thread the water pipe through the hole in the middle of the pebble pool lid and sit it over the base. Feed the end of the water pipe up into the drilled hole in your piece of rock and jam it tightly in place, then sit the rock on the middle of the lid. The 'spare' pipe slides back down into the reservoir. Turn the pump on, and if necessary adjust the water flow rate so that all the water runs back into the reservoir (you'll need to take the lid off the pebble pool to get to the pump to do this – there's a small 'tap' on the pump to adjust the flow rate). If the water doesn't all run back into the reservoir it'll soon empty itself and probably wreck the pump.

11. When you're quite sure everything is okay, spread shingle, small smooth pebbles or, as in this case, cockleshells all over the top of the pebble pool to hide the lid. You can continue it over the surrounding border if you like – its a good way of hiding your electric cable. Plant a few grasses or other sculptural-shaped plants round to complete the effect. Very trendy!

PUTTING IN A PREFORMED PEBBLE POOL BASE

You don't want too much planting round a contemporary water feature like this – a few clumps of something with simple spiky leaves will look perfect. Ornamental grasses or grassy-looking plants are ideal. Plant three of the same about 6 or 8 inches apart to make a striking group – this makes much more impact than dotting ones and twos of lots of different things around all over the place. Sorry about the Latin names – most grasses and sedges don't have common ones. You get used to them; it's like having foreign friends with unusual-sounding names.

Carex hachijoensis **'Evergold'**. A really good green and gold striped evergreen sedge with curving foliage that makes an elegant tuft.

Carex buchananii ▼ An evergreen sedge that looks like a bunch of floppy orange-brown bristles with slightly frizzy ends, very contemporary.

Ophiopogon planiscapus **'Nigrescens'**. Evergreen tufts of short shiny purple-black grassy-looking leaves, with contrasting clusters of tiny purple grape-like fruit on short

stalks in late summer. It's not a grass, but it has narrow strap-shaped leaves that make it look a bit like one.

Helictotrichon sempervirens. Like a steely blue porcupine with tall elegant 'oats' growing out of the middle on long stems in summer. Very pretty indeed, and evergreen.

Miscanthus sinensis **'China'.** A bigger grass with narrow leaves about 3 feet tall topped by red dangling flowers like tassels; very striking. Not evergreen, but it dies down in winter leaving quite an attractive brown skeleton.

KEEPING IT CLEAN

The only thing you've really got to do with a pebble pool is keep it clean. If the water goes green or you get blanket weed, then the pump clogs up. Even if it doesn't, you end up with a disgusting-looking mess with green slime all over your pebbles. The easiest thing to do is to add an algicide to the water. There are lots on the market, so choose the type that suits you best. If in doubt ask for help when you buy it.

* Chemical treatments. These are a bit like the chlorine in swimming-pools, and although they aren't plant- or fish-friendly they won't harm the odd bird that comes to bath in the splash zone. Some of them produce a very slight foaming effect which can actually look good in this type of water feature.

* Plant- and fish-friendly chemicals. These are really intended for use in ponds where you keep fish or grow marginal plants that grow up out of the water, but they are also the kind to use in a pebble pool if you prefer a gentler water treatment or if there are plants growing in the splash zone.

* Biological algicides. The very gentlest kind, as they don't use chemicals at all, but friendly micro-organisms. Unfortunately they are not really practical for very small water features like pebble pools, since the temperature in a small container of water varies so much that the beneficial bacteria can't work well. But if you have a proper pond where there are both fish and plants, that is the place to use this sort of algicide.

TOPPING UP

Pebble pools need topping up occasionally. This is because the water evaporates slowly all the time – it happens faster in hot or windy weather. If your fountain sprays water outside the catchment area, then not all the water runs back into the reservoir so, again, it slowly empties. If the water level in the reservoir runs low, it uncovers the pump, which will eventually burn out. There's no need to dismantle the feature to top it up though. Just run a hosepipe over the top of the pebble pool so the water runs down through the pebbles. You'll know it's full when it overflows.

FOUNTAINS IN BOWLS

There's really nothing to stop you enjoying the sound of running water. It's possible to use a bowl holding as little as half a gallon of water, as long as it's deep enough to cover the pump when you stand it inside. I'd probably use something like a pretty china kitchen bowl, or a plant container – the sort without drainage holes in the bottom are easiest. Then just sit your pump in the bottom of the bowl, fill it with water and switch on. Set the water flow to low, and the ripple it makes is just enough so you don't notice the pump in the water. But what you will have is a bit of cable trailing over the edge of your container – the easiest way to hide this is by putting a few strategically placed potted plants round the water feature.

ELECTRICAL SAFETY

I'm sure I've said it before, but electricity and water are potentially a problem, so always plug pumps or ready-made water features – even if they are the 'safe' low-voltage kind – into a circuit-breaker. This way you are doubly sure. If there's a problem or a cable gets damaged, the power cuts out instantly so you don't get a shock. Plug-in circuit-breakers (Residual Current Devices, RCDs in electrician-speak) cost about £20 from hardware shops and DIY suppliers.

SNAPPY WATER GARDEN

One of the great things about summer is getting home from work while it's still light and getting straight out into the garden. All you want to do at first is sit and soak up the

atmosphere, but after a bit you are ready to wander around with a glass of wine, just enjoying your surroundings. So an occasional new feature is an essential part of your nightly transformation from spaced-out city slicker back to earthling. There are loads of small-but-creative projects you can complete in a few hours over a weekend so you feel you've achieved something, without having to do a lot of heaving hard work. This snappy water garden makes a noticeable change to your surroundings straight away, and with carnivorous plants there's something to watch all summer long. And for some reason men never seem to grow out of the idea that plants that eat flies are cool. I blame *Day of the Triffids*.

Carnivorous plants are fascinating, like rows of open alien mouths waiting to snap something up. Some of them have really weird Martian-type flowers, but their table manners are definitely worth a second look. Because they are bog plants, I like to grow them by the side of a pond where they look really natural and act as natural midge control. If you don't have a pond, just stand a bowl of them on the patio. Because of their weird shapes, you can easily turn a few carnivorous plants into quite an arty arrangement by adding a few natural bog-gardeny sort of extras like a bunch of coloured willow twigs, or some chunks of knobbly driftwood or bogwood.

1. Choose a bowl without drainage holes in the bottom, so you can keep the compost inside nice and boggy. You can sometimes buy special carnivorous-plant compost at big garden centres, otherwise fill the bowl with ordinary peat – don't use normal potting compost because carnivorous plants don't like fertilizer – they prefer their food to fly.

2. Arrange a nice arty chunk of driftwood in the middle, and start planning where to place your plants round it.

3. Tip each plant out of its pot, but don't remove any of the compost from round the roots. This is a venus fly-trap.

4. Scoop out a pot-sized hole in the peat and press the rootball into place just firmly enough to hold the plant upright. I'm planting a pitcher plant, or sarracenia.

5. Put plenty of plants in, using lots of contrasting shapes. Once they are all in, trickle some clean, fine gravel all round them. It's not essential but it looks good.

6. Top the container up to the rim with water so it's nice and boggy. You'll need to trickle the water in slowly from one of those little houseplant watering-cans so the peat and gravel doesn't just mix up and leave you with a bowl of dirty soup. Stand the bowl in a sunny place.

PLANTING UP A BOWL OF CARNIVOROUS PLANTS

CARNIVOROUS PLANTS

Carnivorous plants live naturally in boggy places, where – because there are no nutrients in the peaty soil – they have 'learnt' to feed on flies. Instead of normal leaves, they grow green traps which attract insects and which also act as stomachs to digest them in. Real Hammer horror film stuff! The best carnivorous plants to watch outside in summer are sundews, venus fly-traps and pitcher plants. They each have a different technique for getting dinner.

Venus fly-traps ▼ have hinged leaves with lightning reflexes. When a fly lands on a leaf, the two halves snap together imprisoning the insect inside, turning it into a sandwich.

When the trap opens again a couple of days later the fly looks like it's been hit by a truck. **Pitcher plants** are a bit more subtle. They have long lean traps like bottles. Along comes the fly, sniffs around the top of the trap because there's something nice and sweet inside – you know the way flies are always going round an open bottle of pop? Then it wanders inside for a better look, and once in, it doesn't usually come out again. If you are watching, you think it's been overcome by fumes or lost its footing on the side of the 'bottle', but anyway it falls in, and it's fly soup for supper.

Sundews have little round leaves covered in glistening globules of sticky stuff on stalks. Along comes a fly, lands on a leaf and gets glued to it. The leaf slowly rolls up, taking the fly with it – and when it reopens days later all that's left of the fly is just a dried-out husk. You'd like to think it spits it out, but I'm afraid it doesn't. You can always tell a successful 'hunter' by the bodies stuck to it.

CARNIVOROUS PLANT CARE

In summer. There's no need to feed carnivorous plants as they take care of themselves. But you do need to keep their water level topped up so they are always standing in 1 or 2 inches of water. Save fresh rainwater by leaving a bowl out on the lawn when it's raining, don't use water that may have been stored a long time in a water-butt as you don't know what's got into it. Water out of a pond is okay so long as you haven't used any anti-algae treatment. Otherwise treat tap water to remove the chalk and chemicals, by first running it through a filter jug then boiling it and letting it cool. It's not as much fuss as it sounds – if you filter water anyway to make tea, just save what's left in the kettle afterwards to water your carnivorous plants.

In winter. Carnivorous plants are not quite hardy, so it's not safe to leave them out in the garden in winter. Just bring them indoors and keep them on a cold windowsill, or stand them in a conservatory – it's better for them to be kept well below room temperature, but they shouldn't actually freeze. Whichever way you keep them, they don't look terribly beautiful in winter as the traps go brown – the plants are really only ticking over then. They don't need to stand in water in winter; give them just enough water to stop the compost from drying out.

BOGWOOD

Bogwood is the roots of tropical swamp trees, all twisted and contorted, and very heavy. It looks like it belongs in water somehow, with its peaty colour and black or brown swirls where the knots or the roots come out. You'll find it in aquarium centres, as it is used for decorating fish tanks. Try binding several bits of bogwood together to make a hollow shape to put carnivorous plants in, or take a huge chunk and hollow out the top to make a natural container. Particularly handy is the fact that because it soaks up water, you can stand your bogwood 'container' in a tray of water and as long as you keep the water level topped up the bogwood keeps damp by capillary action.

POTTED PERFECTION

Pot gardening is BIG right now because it's so practical for busy people. When I get home after a busy day at work, I don't want the sort of garden that makes me feel guilty if I'm not fussing over it constantly – it's lovely just to be able to sit and relax if I want to. That's why my garden is mostly paved. There's a huge pergola packed with climbers, and the rest is all containers. I don't grow lots of prissy little plants in small pots that need daily attention. What I like best are more easy-going things that can stay put for years, like my horizontal conifer, which has been in the same container so long it's almost a natural bonsai, and the variegated sedge that lives in my terracotta wall planter.

Working in a garden centre, surrounded by plants, it's impossible not to bring loads of things back home with me. When they get overgrown, I just take them back and we use them for propagating material, so there's always something different to enjoy – but that's the way I like it. I hate the garden to stay the same for too long.

Besides plants, I also collect knick-knacky things I pick up on holiday. There's an ancient griffin that looks really weathered, which I just stand a pot on, and I've got some lovely metal bells on a diamond framework that came from India. Although too many pots just makes lots of watering, too few makes the place look very empty, so combining pots with knick-knacks gives a more decorated look which I like, and makes it easy to change things round. Besides which, it's a great excuse to carry on collecting.

NEW POTS FROM OLD

You don't have to make do with the same old mass-produced plant containers everyone else has got. Instead, why not customize your old ones? It's fun to do, and a great way to amuse yourself on a wet weekend in winter. You can take really beaten-up containers like old plastic pots that have split, or clay pots with a bit missing, and turn them into something new by covering them in fake stone mixture. Don't imagine a potted version of the stone cladding you see on the sort of house you wouldn't want to live in. This is hypertufa, a do-it-yourself version of a naturally porous, holey, craggy form of limestone. When it weathers down, it looks incredibly realistic.

MAKING AND USING FAKE TUFA TO RESURFACE A CONTAINER

Hypertufa is a mixture of cement, sand and peat that you just mix up and slap on. If you aren't over-fussy doing it, when it's dry you get a rough craggy effect that looks brilliant with a bit of moss or lichen growing over it, so I'd give it the yoghurt treatment, the same as for ageing terracotta pots (see page 48).

1. Choose a suitable container and clean it up with a wire brush. You don't want any dust or grease on the outside, so if you need to wash it make sure it's completely dry before moving on to the next stage.
2. Paint a bit of outdoor adhesive over the sides – the idea is to leave little ridges that the coating can grip on to, otherwise it just comes off again. Let it get semi-dry.
3. Mix together equal amounts of peat, sand and cement – a plastic plant pot makes a good measure but it doesn't have to be that exact – you can just tip, say, 2 inches of each ingredient into a bucket. Add water, a little at a time, and mix. It should be a bit thicker than pasta sauce but not as thick as mashed potato.
4. Slap it all over the container, leaving a natural-looking rough surface. Use rubber gloves or an old spoon if you are fussy about your hands.
5. Continue tufa-ing over the rim of the pot and down about an inch inside it, otherwise you'll have a funny-looking bare strip which the compost won't cover when you fill the pot later.
6. Don't move the container until it's really dry, which can take several weeks. With a big heavy container, it's a good idea to coat it where you want to use it so it doesn't need to be moved again.
7. When the surface is touch-dry, fill it with potting compost ready for planting. You'll find its craggy exterior suits rock garden plants or spiky plants.

5

7

MAKING AND USING FAKE TUFA TO RESURFACE A CONTAINER

TUFA TIPS

* A coating of hypertufa is a great way to make a whole lot of tatty old pots instantly match.
* Turn a grotty dark damp back yard into a romantic grotto in just a few hours by coating a breeze-block wall with craggy hypertufa and teaming it with a collection of tufa-clad containers – looks lovely planted up with a few ferns and hostas.

MAKE YOUR OWN TUFA TROUGHS

Antique sinks made of real stone look brilliant for growing rock plants, but they cost a bomb. It's fun making your own out of hypertufa, and lots cheaper. Just make a wire-netting framework by bending small-mesh wire-netting round the bottom and sides of a cardboard box. Use two layers, to make it stronger. Then turn it upside down, leaving the box inside to reinforce the shape, and plaster the outside with hypertufa. Press handfuls of the mixture roughly all over it, so all of the wire-netting is covered about an inch deep. Leave it to dry – it takes several weeks before it is firm enough to move. Then turn it right side up and peel away the soggy remains of the cardboard box where you can. Fill your new trough with potting compost, and plant.

PLANTS TO GROW IN HYPERTUFA CONTAINERS

Because it looks like natural stone, the sort of things that look really good with tufa are slightly wild-looking plants like ferns, rock plants, and some shrubs or conifers. Bedding plants and smart flowers look totally wrong.

Rock plants. A big group of rock plants looks great in a large square stone-effect planter or a huge craggy trough. For single pots, choose drought-proof plants and grow one kind per pot, so you get a big mound of knobbly houseleek (sempervivum) or a thick tuft of sea-thrift.

Conifers. Choose naturally craggy-shaped ones that look almost like bonsai trees. Grow one per pot. Junipers and pines are the safest conifers to grow in pots if you tend to forget the watering, as they are fairly drought-proof. And you can get some beautiful dwarf varieties of both if you only want to use small pots.

Grassy plants. The little black-leaved grassy-looking plant *Ophiopogon planiscapus* 'Nigrescens' is brilliant in a medium-sized pot, or try *Acorus gramineus* 'Variegatus', which has fans of green and gold striped foliage. Any of the festucas, which make blue tussocks, are good in pots too.

Trees ▶ Japanese maple, pictured, is a really good small tree for a pot – you get structural shapes and good foliage, and most kinds have great autumn colour. They even look good in winter, because after the leaves have fallen off you can see the 'skeleton' of twigs.

Hardy trees and shrubs make good all-year-round plants for leaving permanently in tubs, which is much less work than replanting a new lot of annuals every season. You can even grow potentially quite big trees or shrubs in containers because, by keeping the roots confined, the pot keeps them artificially dwarf. Even so, trees and shrubs need quite large containers – at least 12 to 18 inches in diameter – and you need to plant them in soil-based John Innes compost so that they can stay put for years. There's no need to re-pot big shrubs every year, it only needs doing about every 3 to 5 years. Instead, each spring, just top-dress them with fresh potting compost.

1. Scrape off the top couple of inches of compost.
2. Mix your John Innes 3 compost with a small handful of slow-release fertilizer granules, and use it to top up the pot. Leave a 1-inch-deep gap round the rim of the pot, so there's room to water.
3. Water the plant thoroughly to settle the new compost down. Once a plant has been in the same pot for more than a year or so, the container will be well filled with roots so it will need quite a lot of watering.

PAINT EFFECTS

We use a lot of paint on TV when we are making-over gardens. It's very useful when you have to work fast, as you get quick results and it's a lot cheaper than replacing your fences or outbuildings.

Colour makes it easy to give the garden a total 'look' very easily. If you've ended up with a huge mish-mash of different garden furniture, pots, built-in barbecue, pergola poles, arches, decking and so on, you can coordinate the whole lot at one go just by painting them all to match. If you have colour-washed house walls and rendered raised beds you can include them too. You don't have to do everything exactly the same colour – try using different shades of the same colour, like light and dark blue. Blue seems to work well with plants – it really looks good with greens and yellows, though in fact it goes with anything. If you decide on a very multi-coloured look, I'd say just be a bit careful. I reckon you've got to have a pretty good eye to know how to mix a load of violent colours together and make it work.

A lot of people shy off using colour in the garden as they think it's going to look very garish. But you can use it quite subtly, in small doses. The trick is not to over-do it. If you have a family garden, it's great fun to get everybody decorating flower-pots – it's something children enjoy doing, and you can do one from start to finish in an hour or so. It's also very versatile, as you can keep painting over the same pot again and again if it doesn't come out right or you simply fancy a new look. You can paint pots in plain colours, then give them contrasting spots and stripes, or stencil a frieze or flowers over the base coat. Don't worry if the results don't look like they've come out of a factory – I think it's much more fun to have a slightly primitive look, like the sort of paintings children do at school. Again, just get stuck in and see what happens.

USING STENCILS

You can buy stencils, paint, and brushes separately at DIY stores, but if you just want to dabble or if you've only got a couple of containers to do, it's cheaper to buy a kit specially for decorating pots. With any outdoor surface, before you can start the creative stuff you have to spend a few minutes on the boring bits, the preparation, or the paint won't stick. New plastic pots have a very shiny surface that doesn't hold paint very well, so scuff it up a bit by rubbing fine sandpaper over the outside. Wash your containers well in warm soapy water and scrub off any loose dirt or green gunge – a wire brush is good for an old clay pot that is really mucky. Let them dry out completely before putting on any paint. If you want to give a pot a base coat to change the background colour, do this first and wait till it's completely dry before starting to stencil. But it's perfectly okay to apply the paint straight on to bare plastic or terracotta pots. You can seal the pattern in by giving the container a coat of yacht varnish afterwards, but personally I prefer a more primitive, natural look.

1. Stencils work best on flat surfaces, so square pots are easiest to work with. For curved surfaces choose small simple patterns, or use large pots which are easier to tape the stencils round.

2. Choose a suitably sized stencil for the pot. If you use a large pattern like a bunch of grapes, it's best just to do it once, on one side of the pot. Or go for a frieze round the top. Fix the stencil securely in place using masking tape (the sort that peels off again easily without leaving a mark) so it can't slip and smudge your design. If you are using all one colour it's easiest to 'blot' it on with a small sponge – it also makes a nice rough, ready-weathered effect.

3. When you've covered all the holes in the pattern with paint, lift the stencil off carefully so the paint doesn't smudge.

4. Before re-using the stencil on the next part of the container you need to clean and dry it – that's because paint 'creeps' round the edge of the holes, and can smear on where you don't want it. It takes a few minutes, but you get a much better finished result.

5. Stencilling on to bare terracotta gives a nice natural effect that goes well with plants. If you use acrylic paint, the pattern will last a couple of years before it fades – but then you can just wire-brush the pot and start again with a completely new look.

USING STENCILS

SPECIAL EFFECTS

The range of paint products you can buy now is quite amazing, and it's very easy to get effects that used to take hours of messing about by hand. It's lots of fun playing about with paint, and the more you do the better you get, but even your first attempts will look pretty good – so just have a go.

Instant make-over. Restyle plain old clay pots, turning them into something much more exciting, in stripes or spots, for only the price of a tin of paint. Dead easy, and you don't have to be even the tiniest bit artistic.

Distressed. You can make wooden tubs and window-boxes look fashionably distressed, as if they've been out in the weather for years, just by painting them with crackle glaze that you get out of a pot. But I wouldn't over-do it and use it all over your fences and summerhouse as well, or it'll just make the place look neglected.

Verdigris. To make a cheap plastic tub look like verdigris, start by giving it a coat of dark green paint. Then sponge on several shades of blue paint, starting with the darkest first and ending with pale powder-blue. Aim for a lightly stippled effect so that speckles of the previous colours show through.

Metal. You can get metallic paint that makes plastic containers look like brass – when you've painted them, let them dry and smear a tiny bit of gold paint over the sticking-out bits, like the handles on urns, as this makes them look like metal that has worn where it gets handled.

WHICH PAINT?

DIY stores have the biggest choice, and they often sell things like stencils, though you can get a range of decorative garden paints and wood stains in most garden centres now. Artists' suppliers sell all sorts of materials but mostly in tiny quantities, which can work out expensive if you want them for the garden.

Emulsion paint. This doesn't last very long outside – longer if you varnish over it – but it's cheap and you get lots of it for the price, and if you like to change your 'look' every year or two then it's fine. For a distressed look, water it down a bit and brush it on thinly over bare wood or apply thickly and brush over it when it's half dry so you can see the brush-marks.

Acrylics. These are the serious outdoor artist's paints, sometimes described as patio paint, and though they cost more they last longest. Use these for decorating pots with elaborate paint effects or for stencilling if you want the colour to last a long time.

Coloured wood preservatives. These are the ones we use to colour decking, sheds and wooden seats and fences on garden make-overs, and they are good for wooden containers too. They come in a good range of fashionable colours. The brush-on kind is cheapest, but if you have lots of fiddly trellis or bamboo canes to paint it's worth getting the spray version – a bit more expensive but lots quicker.

Masonry paint. You can use ordinary masonry paint, the sort you use for painting rendered house walls, on terracotta pots, and it lasts longer than emulsion. The makers of the ranges of coloured wood stains also now do a matching range of paints for hard surfaces, so you can colour-coordinate pots and metal garden furniture with the rest of the garden.

Varnish. A coat of yacht varnish keeps a painted pot looking fresher longer; wait until the paint has been dry for a few days before varnishing over it.

TOP TIP

AEROSOL PAINTS

Use aerosol paints if you want to give containers an overall background coat fast, or use an aerosol can held at about twice the usual distance from the container to make a light 'mist' of colour. You can apply several light 'mists' of different-coloured aerosol paint one after another for a slightly stippled effect without the bother of sponging. You usually get a more uneven effect, which can be attractive if you like a rougher look. Allow time for each coat to dry before putting on the next, unless you want a slightly more dappled smudgy sort of effect – which can also look good. Experiment on a piece of plain paper first. You can get a range of aerosol paints for use on most hard outdoor surfaces at garden centres and DIY stores.

TOUCH OF THE TROPICS

When I was at college, one of our regular practical tests was to create a foyer display for an office. While the rest of us were making tasteful colour-coordinated pastel displays, one of the students – who came from the Seychelles – would be putting all the loudest colours together to make tropical-style displays. When I suggested it looked a bit over the top, he said no – in a hot country you need strong colours because the light is so intense. We used to argue about it a lot, but it wasn't until I'd travelled more that I started to agree with him.

In Singapore, for instance, I visited the botanic gardens. It was Saturday, the day all the smart weddings go there to have their photographs taken against the most amazing floral and foliage backdrops. They use orchids as bedding plants – don't even think about trying it. There is an avenue of sealing-wax palm trees with vermilion trunks, and a topiary garden full of exotic animals like rhinos grown in tropical creepers over twiggy 'ribs'. There must have been thirty white weddings that day – it was stunning.

At home, a tropical garden look is quite easy to create if you use hardy plants with enormous leaves and really brightly coloured flowers, especially if they also have weird shapes. It helps if you have a few tropical extras, too. A friend of mine keeps pet cicadas and she puts them outside on summer evenings – their singing is straight out of the tropics – and you can get tapes of tropical birdsong. Strong scents, high humidity and bright light all help to give you the full tropical experience – but without the airport delays, lost luggage and (aarrgghh!) holiday vaccinations.

PATIO

When it's sleeting gently and I'm up to my knees in icy water sandbagging the river banks at the garden centre on a cold winter's day, I switch on my favourite daydream. There I am, on my own tropical beach with white sand, something delicious cooking gently over an open fire, and a pool of water to dunk my feet in – no shoes are allowed in this fantasy. But it's quite easy to turn the patio at home into a tropical paradise just by using the right plants, decorations and furnishings. Anyone can do it. It's great fun to play around with ideas, and even more fun to come home to a tropical evening cooking, eating and drinking in the garden. There are all sorts of ethnic accessories that help to set the scene – Balinese wood-carvings, Cambodian cooking-pots, the temple bells type of wind-chimes, cane chairs, bamboo screens, tribal rugs and throwovers slung over benches. If you've got paving, break it up with a few woven mats and squashy cushions on the ground. After all, this is a sprawly kind of garden – you are supposed to feel laid back and relaxed.

PLANTS TO GIVE A PATIO A TROPICAL TOUCH

I'd want a tropical-style patio to look like a clearing in the jungle. To get this effect, go for a few really big jungly-looking creepers up the walls or on a pergola and let them just twine together for a really lush look. That's really all you need to get the look, plantwise, but if you don't mind going to the effort of watering a few tubs you could add just a few tender exotic flowers or big feature plants.

Tender exotic flowers ▶ The patio is the place for a few really bright, colourful, tropical-look perennials that need bringing in for the winter. Cannas, pictured, are really tropical-looking, with great big red or orange flowers and huge leaves; in winter they die down to tubers that you need to keep almost dry. *Salvia grahamii* is a bushy slightly tender plant with lots of smallish bright red flowers and leaves that smell like blackcurrant if they get bruised. Keep cuttings on the windowsill indoors in winter if you don't have room for a big plant. *Lobelia cardinalis* 'Queen Victoria' is a bog plant with purple-red leaves and bright red flowers, good in pots but needs to be kept very wet. Hardy in mild areas.

Palms. If you live in a mild area there are several almost hardy palms you can use, like *Chamaerops humilis* and *Trachycarpus fortunei* – that's the one you see growing outside in Cornwall. Their big leafy look is straight out of the jungle.

Climbers. Anything with big leaves like *Vitis coignetiae* is good, and you'll want a few nice wafts of scent from trachelospermum or jasmine. I'd also add the evergreen *Clematis armandii*, which has stunning leaves and scented flowers in spring, so you get to keep your tropical touch all year round.

Tropical-look perennials. Go for alstroemeria – the new patio kinds are short, ideal for pots, and have masses of lily-like flowers in lots of colours. They keep flowering right through the summer if you keep tugging the dead flower-stems out. In winter, though they are hardy, sink the pots to their rim in a bed of soil for insulation – they don't like to be too wet either.

TOP TIP

SPECIAL EFFECTS

If you don't have real tropical sun or surroundings, just fake it. The great thing about using paint in the garden is that you can create all sorts of 'special effects'.

Instant sunshine. If you have a really tiny, shut-in garden surrounded by dark walls, painting them sky blue immediately opens it up and makes it look as if the sun is shining all the time.

Disguise your eyesores. If there's an ugly shed you can either make it vanish by painting it holly green and surrounding it with foliage, or turn it into a beachcomber's hut by painting it a fashionable shade of blue and putting some built-in seating or a bit of decking in front of it.

Making an impression. You don't have to be at all artistic to paint blobs of colour Monet-style to suggest a livid sunset on the back wall of the shed, or foliage and flowers on a wall.

TOP TIP

CHEAT'S EXOTICS

If you don't want the bother of trying to keep tender plants through the winter, or the cost of replacing them every year, again, you can always cheat. Just move your houseplants outside for the summer. Don't try it with real, delicate tropical plants, but the tougher things like weeping fig, indoor yuccas and cordylines, bromeliads, spider plants, and asparagus fern will actually love being used as temporary patio plants. The change does them good and the odd shower really freshens them up. Stand them in big ethnic-style tubs or troughs, and pour cocoa-shell in between the pots. This is lovely stuff, like loads of little soft bark-like flakes – you buy it in bags at garden centres. It not only makes the plants look more jungly, but it also stops the roots over-heating and drying out so fast. Unfortunately, when you first spread cocoa-shell around, it smells of dark chocolate and always triggers an instant chocolate crisis with me. One sniff, and I've got to get my teeth into a bar of the stuff. Thank goodness that as cocoa-shell weathers it changes to a nice earthy tropical rainforest scent which doesn't send you screaming to the nearest sweet shop.

TUFA GARDEN IN A TRAY

If you are feeling adventurous, you could make up an oriental rock garden based on an original idea I 'borrowed' from a garden in Singapore. They had a big chunk of natural tufa rock with 2 or 3 bonsai plants growing in it. It looked really good. At home you could do the same thing, but I'd use an indoor bonsai tree. That way you can stand it on the patio in summer if you want, and then take it indoors for the winter so it doesn't get too cold. (Normal bonsais are a problem, because they need winter protection but being outdoor trees they aren't happy indoors.) Real tufa rock is essential for this project – you can get it from alpine plant specialists and bonsai nurseries. What's special about real tufa is that it is porous so it soaks up water, and it is also soft and spongy so you can make holes and plant things straight into it – the roots grow right into the rock.

1. Turn your chunk of tufa round to see which way it looks best. If it won't stand up straight, use a saw to cut a bit off the bottom to give it a level base. Sit it down in soft ground or on any flat surface while you work on it. Dig out a little planting pocket using a hammer and chisel or an old screwdriver. Take it easy – you don't want to shatter the rock.
2. Buy an indoor bonsai tree – this one is a podocarpus, which has been specially trained with a kink in its stem so it looks old and craggy. Remove any loose soil from the roots after taking the plant out of its pot – you can just tease it away with your fingers.
3. Tuck the roots into the planting pocket in your rock along with a little potting compost. The plant should look as if it's growing naturally in a crevice just like it would in wild rocky landscape. Finally, stand the planted piece of tufa in a tray and top it up with water. Because it's porous, moisture is automatically drawn up through the rock and keeps the plant watered. If you stand the rock feature off-centre in its tray, the water makes a 'mountain pool' in front of it, which looks brilliant.

TUFA GARDEN IN A TRAY

WHAT HAPPENS IN WINTER?

It's very difficult to keep a patio looking tropical in winter, when your indoor plants have to go back indoors and palm trees and so on need protecting from frost. But there are ways. You could take a tip from some garden contractors I know. They planted a scheme outside an office block some time ago, and it looked great until all the plants died off in winter. Rather than explaining that that's what most perennial plants normally do, they went back and put some new plants in, which this time stayed in flower all year round. The company was delighted, until one day they found the guys taking the flowers away – to be cleaned. For two years, nobody had noticed that their flowers were actually made of silk!

Serious gardeners tut-tut like crazy if you even mention silk flowers, but with something like a tropical garden you are creating an illusion anyway, so it wouldn't worry me for a moment to cheat. If silk flowers are that good – and there are some really brilliant ones around – that's the way to make a tropical garden stay tropical in winter. If you were really strapped for time, you could even use them all year round on your patio, with just a few big, real, climbers for background.

CONTINUING THE THEME INDOORS

When you've made yourself a really brilliant tropical garden outside, the last thing you want is to peek in through the patio doors and see a terribly English interior. The two just don't jell. I'd prefer to make a more gradual transformation by standing cane furniture or a tin trunk just inside the house, and standing indoor plants on it. If you've got a conservatory that is kept at room temperature in winter, you can go to town with a really spectacular tropical scheme using water and exotic plants in there. And a conservatory is just the place to keep all your tender tropical-look patio plants that can't be left outdoors in winter.

* Grow a few big plants like coconut palm, weeping fig and Swiss cheese plant – they take less looking after, but make more of an impression than lots of little ones. Big specimens don't cost a bomb if you buy them in supermarkets – that way you can afford to change them regularly so you don't get fed up with them.
* Hang a few colourful Balinese wood-carvings in the branches if your plants are big enough – parrots or one of those tropical fish mobiles might be fun.
* Put up rattan blinds to give a tropical touch and to prevent plants from scorching in the bright sunlight, and to keep the temperature more comfortable in summer. A big slow-running circulator fan up in the roof helps too. Just like the Raffles Hotel.
* Make an indoor pool, which can be a small water tank from a DIY store with cork stuck over. Or just bring your potted pond into the conservatory for the winter, when it's too cold to keep it on the patio.

* If you want a really authentic rainforest feeling, make a tropical 'mist'. To do this you need to get a small mister unit – they sell them for orchid growers, and you often find them at aquarium centres. Plug it in and it will give you a small mist cloud that looks great hovering among the leaves. It's really good for tropical plants.

REALLY WILD ICE-BUCKET

I saw this done at a party out in New Zealand last time I was there; it looks great and it's really easy to do as long as you have room in your freezer and start thinking about it a couple of days beforehand. Or you can make it really well in advance and just leave it in the freezer until it's needed.

1. Pick a mixture of perfect-looking leaves and flowers – edible flowers like borage, violets, nasturtiums and chives are good, and you can pick the petals off calendula marigolds, but since you aren't actually going to eat them you can use whatever you like.
2. Get a big plastic soft drinks bottle and cut off the top.
3. Put a 1 to 2 inch layer of ice cubes in the bottom of a small plastic bucket. Stand your decapitated bottle in the middle of the bucket on the ice and surround it with petals. The ice cubes help to keep the petals in place when you pour in the water as well as enabling it to freeze more quickly.
4. Put some stones or gravel in the bottle-base to weight the bottle down, then pour water into the bucket to come half-way up the sides of the bottle. Put it in the freezer until the water is frozen solid.
5. Once it's frozen, fill the sides of the bucket with more ice, water and petals up to the rim, then freeze it solid again. For an even brighter version, fill the bucket by making and freezing lots of layers, each with a different colour petal.
6. Just before the party, take the bucket out of the freezer. Tip out the gravel, then pour a little hot water into the soft drinks bottle and stand the outer bucket in hot water for a few minutes so you can separate them, leaving a real ice bucket 'shell' studded with petals. Although it will have a flat bottom it can still slide a bit on a table, so try standing it on a cloth. It looks really pretty on a meal table, and takes ages to melt.

REALLY WILD ICE-BUCKET

ENTERTAINING IN STYLE

Cooking even the simplest food outdoors somehow feels a little exotic. But while barbecues are a great option, it's also worth thinking about a terracotta bread oven. I've seen them in Portugal for years, but now they are over here too. A bread oven looks like a terracotta kiln with a chimney, and there's a hole in the front where they used to put the bread tins on a bed of wood ashes. You can fuel it with charcoal and cook over the embers just like a barbecue, and you can also smoke meat or fish in the chimney part. The real beauty of it, though, is that the terracotta walls glow with warmth for quite a while after you finish cooking, so that as night falls you can still sit out, snuggled up in rugs and watching the bats flitting round.

Whether you use a bread oven or a barbecue, you can jazz up your cooking with a few exotic touches.

* Try wrapping meat in big edible grape leaves or French sorrel, from your garden, as living tinfoil when you barbecue it, and putting a few scented twigs on the charcoal – use eucalyptus, dried vine prunings, or the tough stems from herbs after you've used the leaves in a recipe.

* Or for a really tropical effect drip a few drops of any exotic aromatherapy oil on to the embers; I like tea tree oil, but any of the citrus, conifer or exotic flower oils would be good. It gives an ordinary barbecue the atmosphere of a Fijian beach party.

FLOATING CANDLES

Floating candles give your outdoor dinner party an instantly exotic touch. The first time I saw floating candles was in India, when I was eighteen and I took a boat trip down the Ganges. There was a festival going on, and they were floating short lighted candles downstream on bits of tinfoil surrounded by marigold petals. It looked gorgeous. Next

time you want something very simple for a table-centre decoration at your dinner party, or just dotted around your patio in the evening to add a bit of romance, why not try something similar.

* Just float some candles in a bowl of water. You can buy all sorts of floating candles now – they do some shaped like flowers.

* Ordinary tea-lights will float if you sit them on small squares of cork (cut up a cork tile), with a pin through the base to hold the candle in place, and then use flowers or small leaves to hide the cork.

SECRET GARDEN

At the water garden centre, there's a path that leads down to a 'secret' place by the river where nobody goes much because it's a bit overgrown and you have to push your way through the branches to get there. It's a real jungle. It just needs a bench to be perfect, but it's a lovely place to stop and watch the water go by. That's where I usually see the kingfisher.

Nowadays everybody needs a quiet corner where they can escape from the world for a while. You don't need a big area – you can tuck a secret garden away behind a dense screen of shrubs in a tiny space, or turn a whole small town garden into an exotic hideaway.

The trick to getting a tropical jungle look is to have loads of really big glossy leaves and some cane stems. It doesn't matter what they are or how you mix them together so long as they are huge and jungly. It's amazing how many enormous leaves you can find among perfectly hardy plants. Even laurel works, if it's in the right sort of surroundings. And lots of perennials have huge leaves too.

HARDY PLANTS WITH TROPICAL LOOKS

Miscanthus is the next best thing to sugar cane, and looks like a giant grass about 6 feet tall which goes brown in winter but stays looking nice and jungly even so.

Fatsia japonica has big thick shiny fig-shaped leaves, but because it's evergreen the effect lasts all year round, so it makes a great background plant for jungly effects. It flowers in early winter, which is just when you want them, but they are odd rather than stunning.

Clerodendrum trichotomum fargesii is the must-have tropical-look tree; it's quite small, not much more than a shrub with a single stem, but it has big heart-shaped leaves, and really exotic scented maroon and white flowers in late summer followed by blue berries in autumn.

The **'hardy' banana (*Musa basjoo*)** is worth risking in mild areas. It has really enormous leaves and a great tall stem that dies down every winter.

Big-leaved perennials. Lots of bog plants have big leaves – think of gunnera, and *Darmera peltata*, which has big round leaves that look like parasols. If you don't have a damp spot, go for plume poppy (macleaya), which has tall stems of big grey-green leaves and big coral plumes of flower.

Bamboo ◄ goes great with anything big and leafy, as the long thin stems make such a good contrast of shapes. It's also very easy to grow anywhere that's not too wet or windy, and it does well in big containers. Most of the popular kinds are quite slow-growing.

AVOIDING WEEDS

They don't have weeds in real rainforest, but there's a very good reason for that. The trees grow quite close together and they go straight up for over 100 feet. It's an amazing feeling standing underneath looking up, because they blot out all the light so you can't see the sky. Because it's so dark at ground level, seedlings can't grow until an old tree falls down and lets the sunlight in. So the floor of the forest is all just leaf litter. At home, you won't be able to get your plants thick enough to give you total freedom from weeding, but, as ever, there are ways round this.

* Before planting your jungle, get the ground ready and then cover it with anti-weed matting – this is a woven plastic fabric which acts as a weed-proof membrane. You can buy it in garden centres. Perforated black polythene does the same job but isn't so strong.
* Just unroll the sheet and peg it down over the soil. You can get special pegs for the job, or just use U-shaped bits of bent wire, prong end down, to spear it to the soil. Where you want to put a shrub, cut a cross in the fabric and lift the corners back.
* After planting, tuck the flaps back round the plant, and cover the finished bed with a couple of inches of bark chippings. You'll never need to weed again!

DEALING WITH OVERGROWN SHRUBS

Most trees and shrubs go for years without needing pruning, but when your jungle gets too lush for its own good, just tidy it up a bit – though with this style of garden it's important not to overdo it, as you don't want to spoil the Tarzan effect. You can use the same technique to rejuvenate a normal overgrown garden, but there you can afford to go at it a bit harder. The very best time to hack shrubs back is in spring, as that's when they start growing again, but if you're desperate to make the garden look better straight away I'd take the risk and do it whenever you feel like it. Apart from a few trees and shrubs that stand hacking back completely, like the dogwoods and willows with coloured stems which I've talked about elsewhere, don't chop a whole shrub back to the ground – even if you don't actually kill it, you'll stop it flowering for several years while it gets its act back together. What you are aiming at is simply to restore the natural shape of the plant. The golden rule is never to cut out more than one quarter of a shrub in one year.

1. First stand back and take a good look at your shrub. Some plants need only a lightish 'haircut' to get them back in shape. The idea is to remove any sticking-out bits that spoil the shape, but don't just snip off lots of little bits all over the place, it's much better to cut a complete stem right back close to the main trunk of the plant. This way the cut-off bits are hidden by leaves, so the plant doesn't look butchered and you aren't left with lots of sharp sticks poking out dangerously.

2. Cut any really old, damaged, balding or generally nasty-looking branches off as close to the ground as possible. This encourages new shoots to grow out from the bottom of the plant, so it soon thickens up, and it's a brilliant way to rejuvenate old neglected shrubs or to thin out overcrowded ones. Do it over several years, taking out a quarter of the stems each time and starting with the worst, or the oldest ones, first. (You can always tell the oldest branches of a shrub because the bark is darker than on the new shoots, and it is often craggy-looking instead of smooth.)

DEALING WITH OVERGROWN SHRUBS

1

LOST WORLDS

A jungle always makes me imagine that at any moment I could stumble over the remains of a lost civilization. You could capture the same feeling at home with a bit

of fallen stone pillar, or a broken bit of statue half pushed over, with a tangle of climbers growing over it.

* You can get some very ethnic-looking 'heads' a bit like the ones on Easter Island, except these are small and hollow so you can plant things in them – they're really great with grasses, which look like the 'hair'. You could sit two or three on a rough wooden shelf, like ju-ju idols.
* A few creatures crawling in and out of the jungle would be good too – a stone crocodile coming up out of a big puddle of water, or a slate iguana or gecko just emerging from under a big leaf. It all adds to the atmosphere.
* Or just have a browse through a reclamation yard and see what you can find.

PLANTING THE INTERIOR

Once you've got a thick jungly framework round the edge of your retreat, you want a few tropical-looking flowers you can only see from inside it.

Hardy hibiscus are nice neat shrubs with enormous exotic flowers like the indoor hibiscus but in different colours – you can get mauve, blue, pink or red and white flowers, but not orange, red or yellow. They are no work at all.

Lilies can look quite tropical in a big-leafy setting. Tiger lilies would be brilliant – big orange trumpet flowers with black dots. Some lilies have really big heavily scented flowers with a raised pattern of bumps on the petals, which makes them look and smell very exotic – this kind are actually called oriental hybrids.

Subtropical border ► A splash of hot bright colour really packs a punch, but keep it small so you don't make yourself a whole lot of work. Go for all the reds and oranges, with a few bits of purple and yellow: crocosmia, pictured, big single red dahlias like 'Bishop of Llandaff', cannas, and loud bedding plants like coleus and castor oil plant (ricinus). These are all tender plants that need winter protection, or, in the case of bedding, need replacing early each summer.

OTHER IDEAS

TREE ART

* You can cut a spyhole through a hedge to look into your secret garden from the outside – that's the place to put a statue half strangled by climbers.
* Or make a tribal archway – take a bendy tree sapling and curve it into an arch, held in place with wire until it 'sets' into shape. This would make a great natural entrance between two big banks of jungly foliage.
* One thing that looks very tropical is to take a big-leaved tree like a paulownia or catalpa and hack it back hard every year or two. Instead of growing into a huge tree you wouldn't have room for, you get several short strong stems with really huge leaves instead.
* If you wanted to be a bit arty, after your hacked-back paulownia or catalpa tree starts to grow new shoots you could plait three of them together and cut off the rest, so you have a twisty tree sculpture. The good thing about this is that after a couple of years the tree would need hacking back again, so you could do something different with it next time.

TOP TIP

HANGING OUT

One thing I'd have to have in my secret garden is a hammock. They're so relaxing. You're just gently rocked off to sleep. You can't beat it. Hammocks on stands just aren't the same, so if you are going to get a hammock make sure you've got somewhere to hang it – trees are best. Otherwise you can use strong poles cemented into the ground. Try to put your hammock somewhere where there are plants underneath. It just feels so much more comfortable than a hammock strung up over hard paving. And it would be lovely to drift off with some nice herby scents wafting up round you.

LET RIP

On the way back from New Zealand, I stopped off in Hong Kong to visit the famous Chinese garden that they made in the 1970s. When it was new, it was *the* big thing to see, but by the time I got there the place had been neglected for years. The plants were half wild, some of the ornaments had almost vanished in foliage and the shape of the garden was blurred with overgrown creepers. It was magic.

I'm entranced by that feeling of faded glory you get when you visit an old garden that has once been really something but has been left to slowly go downhill, where you are always stumbling over long-forgotten features or pushing through overgrown plants. It feels really nostalgic – that 'lost garden' atmosphere is terribly romantic.

I love browsing in second-hand shops and junk yards because it gives you the opportunity for re-creating this sort of feeling deliberately. When you see battered old furniture or bits of broken junk just piled up in a heap, you somehow forget what it was once used for and start dreaming up ways to give it a new life. Before you know it, you've bought all kinds of rubbish and your friends think you're mad. Once you are a junk-spotter, you can see the hidden possibilities in all sorts of things.

The grottier the junk, the cheaper it is. I love the idea of recycling what other people don't want any more or turning everyday objects into something unexpected. You can easily make glossy magazine-style garden features for next to nothing – the sort of thing that will make your friends say, 'So that's what happened to your old central heating boiler.' All it takes is imagination and a bit of paint.

RECYCLING IN ACTION

Any garden needs a touch of the unexpected, and the smaller the garden, the more badly it needs it. One garden I visited had a bunch of women's arms sticking out of the ground, complete with long red-painted finger-nails. Talk about shock. My first thought was they had buried a body. I suppose it's not really my sort of thing, but in an odd sort of way, it worked. It pulled you up short and sharpened you up for the rest of the garden.

Small gardens can turn out to be very predictable. That's one reason why I'm so keen on do-it-yourself garden art. You can recycle almost anything as garden art, even if you don't own a welding set, and make really novel 'surprise' features. It's cheap, fun, and very easy to do.

Home-made art can often turn out better than the real thing. When you fall in love with a piece of sculpture at a studio you assume that because it's expensive it will automatically look really good in the garden at home, so it's very disappointing if it doesn't. The great thing about making your own art is that it's cheap, so if it doesn't turn out right it's no big hassle to try again. It's amazing what you can come up with if you try. And often just by accident. So get stuck in and see what happens.

WIND-CHIMES MADE FROM KNIVES AND FORKS

Wind-chimes are great in gardens. If you don't have running water, the sound they make is a nice alternative and it's very relaxing. Don't put chimes in the windiest part of the garden or they'll drive you – and the neighbours – potty. Instead, put them where there is an occasional waft of wind so you just get a gentle tinkling sound – they are lovely hanging from the branch of a tree. You can buy wind-chimes in garden centres. Those with wooden or large metal pipes make a lower note; small metal pipes make a higher sound. But it's very easy to make your own – you can drill holes through some copper pipes of different lengths, then hang them from fishing line. And a really nice idea I saw recently was for wind-chimes made of old silver cutlery.

1. **Collect some old knives, forks and spoons from a junk shop – they don't need to match.**
2. **Hammer some of the spoons flat to make them look a bit different.**

3. Bend some of the prongs of the forks and jam a pebble or a glass marble in between others.

4. You can always add a dab of glue to make sure your bead or marble can't drop out – use clear silicon so it doesn't show.

5. Tie a length of fishing line to each piece of cutlery.

6. By screwing in a hook, fix some chain to a flat-edged bit of log and secure the dangling bits of cutlery on their fishing lines all round the edge of it to make a chandelier type of effect. I've just draped them around and tied them, but you can easily secure them with tacks or a staple-gun.

7. Hang the finished chimes up. The individual pieces of cutlery are far enough apart to stop them constantly jangling, and the tree where I've hung them is a little distance away from a seating area, so all you get are occasional faint tinkling sounds – just right!

WIND-CHIMES MADE FROM KNIVES AND FORKS

CONTAINER ART

All sorts of offbeat things can be used to hold plants – the odder the better.

* Once when I was on holiday in France I drove past a place with loads of old shoes lined up along a wall – stilettos, trainers, sensible brogues and all sorts – all planted up with bedding plants; it looked lots of fun.
* An old bath looks great painted blue, with plants standing on stones inside it.
* Kitchen pots and pans, wooden crates, buckets and birdbaths all make good plant containers – you name it, you can plant something in it.
* If you fancy using something that doesn't hold soil, like a basket or a colander, you can always either line it with black polythene, like you would a hanging basket, or just use it to stand a potted plant inside – tuck some moss or bark chippings round the pot to hide it, and nobody will ever know.

THE SECRET OF SUCCESS

The secret of making garden art look stunning is to place it right, but there's no need to make a great fuss. Just plonk it down. Try it in several different places before making up your mind. You can always shift it again when you want to make-over that bit of the garden.

* Most garden art, and especially the homemade sort, tends to look better if it's slightly hidden or you come across it round a corner, so it looks as if it's almost erupted naturally among the leaves.
* A tall bit of art is good for stopping you looking straight to the end of a flat garden, and you could use it as a support for a big climber later.
* To stop a heavy ornament slowly sinking into soft soil or tipping over, stand it on a paving slab. To give a small piece more prominence, raise it up on a plinth, which could be made of a pile of bricks with a paving slab on top, or perhaps a log set on end in the soil.

INSTANT ART

Garden art doesn't have to be terribly exotic. In fact, it's often a case of the simpler the better. There are loads of things you can do with stuff you pick up from the builder's merchants or scrap yards for just a few pounds.

* A few bits of copper water pipe, hammered into the ground at an angle, can look good behind the right plants (see facing page).
* Air-ducting pipe is brilliant. It's just silvery grey pipe with a spiral up it – you can find it at junk shops, where it's been taken out of buildings. Chop it to different lengths and slip them over posts to make them stand up wherever you want them.

* Concrete-reinforcing bars have a nice twist, like barley-sugar, and bend easily into all sorts of angular shapes you can just stick in anywhere. They look even better when they rust, or you could spray-paint them.

OTHER IDEAS

LAND ART

Land art is a good option, and great fun too. Don't be put off by the name, it's just called that because it goes on the ground. It's an interesting and easy way of filling part of the garden where nothing much grows, where it's very shady or the soil is awful. It's certainly a lot easier than trying to improve the conditions so plants will grow. And you can really indulge in a bit of fantasy too. Just remember, when you feel like a change, you can always re-use the original materials in a new way.

Big beasts. You can make a brilliant serpent by pushing bits of old broken roofing tiles into gravel – the scaly shapes make quite a realistic-looking crest down the back. You can do dragons and Loch Ness monsters too. The trick is to copy a picture from a book – trickle fine sand down to mark out the shape you want, then fill it in with tiles. If you try to work free-hand you'll just end up in a mess.

Do-it-yourself dig. On one of my trips to New Zealand I went to a garden that had a really dark shady corner with horrible trashy soil. Instead of trying in vain to grow plants there, the owners just dug out a big hole and put in two or three garden ornaments so it looked like they were excavating an archaeological dig. It looked fantastic. They used copies of the terracotta warriors from China, but you could do it with anything, even old dirty or broken concrete statues. Remember, though – for this to look good, it mustn't end up giving the idea you've started a rubbish tip down the garden!

TOP TIP

JUNK FOR FREE

You don't always have to go out and buy junk, because most of us have plenty of our own that we've never quite got round to slinging out – and because we've walked past it every day for years we don't always spot its potential. Give it a new home, a new use and a new coat of paint – spray paint is the answer for tricky shapes – and away you go.

OTHER IDEAS

BROODY BASKETS

Old hanging baskets are really useful too. Most people just throw them away when they look a bit battered or the wire ones go rusty, but they are good for turning into frames for training 'topiary' – you can use the basket shape upside down and add bits of wire to make heads or tails. They make great broody hens or peacocks. Or wire two hanging baskets together to make a sphere, which looks terrific planted with ivies to make a green globe. The ivy covers the shape within a few months.

ADVICE FROM THE SHED FAIRY

* Old vegetable racks are very practical for storing all sorts of things in a shed as they let the dirt fall through. They are good for putting small things into so they don't get lost, like knives, labels and string. I find them very handy for trowels – you want to keep them just inside the door where you can get hold of them quickly.

* A tatty old bristly doormat nailed up on the shed wall is a good way of cleaning garden tools after you've used them: just give them a scrub against it as you go past.

NEW WATER FOR OLD

You don't have to keep a water feature looking the same for ever. You might have inherited a pond along with your garden, or maybe you put in a pebble pool a while ago and just fancy giving it a mini make-over. It's a lot easier to do than you think. If you've got a pond, the best time to alter it is when it needs a clear-out – just changing the plants gives it an instant lift. And you can give your pebble pool a new look whenever you like just by putting something different on top for the water to come out of. It's quick, fun, and you can keep using the same basic kit over again in lots of different ways.

ALTERING YOUR PEBBLE POOL

If you already have a pebble pool, you can give it a brand new look in a couple of hours just by changing the ornament on top. Water garden centres sell a range of jugs, urns and jars all ready to fit in place – no hassle. But if you don't mind taking a risk you can adapt the ornament of your choice by drilling a hole in it wide enough to take a water pipe. The trick is to use a masonry drill at low speed; use a small diameter drill-bit first and then enlarge it by using a wider drill to bore out the same hole. Even if you are terribly careful there's always a chance you'll crack the container – which is why the ones you buy ready drilled cost so much more than plain pots. You are paying for the ones they break, too!

1. **This pebble pool originally had the water welling up through a drilled rock. I've just lifted the rock out, leaving the plastic water pipe coming up from the pump all ready to push up into a new ornament. You don't need to disturb the rest of the pool at all.**

2. This urn has been made specially to use as a water feature. The flattened bit near the base means it will lie on its side without rolling over. It came with a couple of holes drilled near the base – the two different sizes are so you can choose the one that's the right diameter for your water pipe, and just block up the other one. Plug it with clear silicon, or jam a pebble or a cork in first and seal round it with silicon. A lot of people like to use glazed ceramic containers or terracotta pots meant for plants, and you can use the same technique to fill unwanted drainage holes in the bottom to 'convert' them into jars for a pebble pool.

3. Once the silicon is dry, get someone to hold the container over the pebble pool while you thread the water pipe in through the hole, and carry on exactly the same as if you were making a pebble pool first time round. (Check out your technique in the watery chapter 'Wet, Wet, Wet', page 151.)

ALTERING YOUR PEBBLE POOL

ALTERNATIVE TOPS

Once you have got a small pebble pool base sunk into the ground, you can keep changing the look just by putting a different ornament on top for the water to come out of.

* Try drilling through the centre of a pottery plate. The water makes a ripple running out from the middle of the plate as if you've thrown a stone into a bucket of water, then it runs off over the edge, back through the stones into the reservoir.

* A chunk of bogwood or tufa rock, drilled through the middle so the water wells up out of the top and trickles down the sides, makes a really natural-looking water feature for a wilder-style garden. Since tufa and bogwood both soak up water, you could actually plant a fern or rock plant into it. You'll have to make a hole for the plant to go into, but both tufa and bogwood are reasonably soft so it's not difficult to do.

* You often find stalls at county shows selling second-hand gardening tools – that's where I find old watering cans. One of these looks great tucked into an odd corner, so it looks like it was abandoned years ago. But if you drill through the base and have running water spilling out into a pool of pebbles, it adds to the sense of 'dilapidated garden' charm.

* Another good one is a standpipe with an old tap that is constantly running slowly – you can have it running into an old bucket that in turn overflows into pebbles if you like. It looks like the gardener got called away in a hurry.

REINVENT YOUR POND

If you've got a pond, then by the time it's been there for five years or so all the plants in and around it will be getting definitely overgrown and loads of sludge will have built up in the bottom. Time for a clear-out. If you are starting over again completely and getting rid of all your old plants, you can do it any time between spring and late summer. But if you are going to split and re-pot some of the existing plants, you've really got to do this job in spring even though there will be tadpoles around, so the new plants still have time to grow, flower and get settled in the same year. Water-lilies just rot if they are disturbed late in the year.

* There's no need to run the 'old' water out. Although it's a bit messy, it's much better to muck out a pond leaving the old, matured water in it. Pond water is like wine – it improves with age. New tap water is full of chemicals and nutrients, which is why it takes a new pond so long to get in balance with nature.

* Just lift out all your old water plants – they should be growing in planting baskets, so apart from you getting wet it's quite easy to do. Swill them round a bit in the water as you lift them out, to dislodge any tadpoles or baby fish.

* If there are any you want to re-use, get them out of their baskets, divide them up and replant one good piece back into the same basket using special aquatic soil, which you get from water garden centres.
* Then treat yourself to a new set of plants. A new set of plants lets you change the theme of a pond at a stroke. You might go from rather wild-looking plants like kingcups, bogbean and brooklime to an altogether smarter set like peltandra and floating water hyacinths for a more tropical look. Re-pot new water plants from the tiny pots they are sold in into bigger baskets about 9 inches square, using the special aquatic soil.
* While the pond is clear of plants, you could take the opportunity to change your fountain or put in some underwater lighting if you want to.
* It's not much fun, but you need to get rid of some of the sludge. Use a big jam-jar and carefully scoop out some of the black goo that settles in the bottom of the pond, so there's only about a 2- or 3-inch layer left. The stuff you take out is good to spread on a border or put on the compost heap. Then put your new plants back in, and leave everything to settle down.

FISH

* If you are going to keep fish, you need a pond at least 18 inches and better still 2 feet deep, as deep water stays warmer so fish can survive the winter outside. You must also have plenty of oxygenating plants like elodea pondweed or water violet, and ideally a few other water plants growing in baskets, as this gives the fish lots of places to hide.
* The best fish for a small easily maintained garden pond are goldfish or shubunkins. They are colourful and friendly, and won't grow too big for comfort. Buy fish over 2 inches long – the very small ones don't have a high survival rate when they are moved.
* Don't put too many in – you only want 1 inch of fish to every square foot of pond surface. If they are happy they'll breed.
* Introduce new fish to a pond carefully. Don't just tip them straight in. Float the bag they are sold in on top of the pond for half an hour so the temperature adjusts to that of the pond, then untie the end and let some pond water in. After another 5 minutes duck the open end of the bag under water so they can swim out.
* Feed the fish from spring to late summer if you want them to get tame and spend more time on the surface where you can see them – it doesn't matter if you don't

feed them as they'll still get plenty of wild food that turns up naturally in the pond, like water fleas and mosquito larvae.

* To save fish from herons, cover the pond with a net or put a trip wire about 6 inches high all round it in winter and spring. Herons are actually most dangerous to fish in spring, when they have babies to feed, so don't relax your precautions till late May.

ROUTINE POND CARE

IN SPRING

* Divide any overgrown marginal plants, about every 3 years. Lift them out of their baskets, tip them out and divide them just like a herbaceous plant in a border, then replant one bit in new pond soil, and put it back in the pond. Give the rest away or plant them in a bog garden.
* Don't disturb water-lilies more than you have to; they need re-potting only about every 5 to 7 years. And don't grow them where they will get splashed by a fountain or waterfall – this is one of the commonest reasons why they don't do well. They like their leaves to stay dry on top.
* Fountains clog up fairly regularly in summer. If you use one with a pebble pool and you put algicide in the water you'll hardly have any problems as the water stays so clean; but in a pond where the pump sucks up algae, weed and muck, the holes in the fountain jet often get blocked so you need to take the fountain head off when that happens and poke something like the tip of a cocktail stick through the holes to clean them out. You'll also need to clean the filter on your pump, if it's the sort that has one, perhaps as often as once a week.

IN WINTER

* Unless you are going to leave a pump running all winter, it's best to take it right out of the pond, then clean and dry it and store it somewhere dry and frost-free like indoors. If it's left in water but not working it can seize up, and it'll do the same if you take it out but leave it dirty or damp.
* Cover the pond with a net in autumn to keep leaves out of the water, then if herons are a problem leave the net in till spring to keep your fish safe.

GONE TO POT

Mosaic can look amazing, and it's great fun to do. As well as the usual sort made from pieces of broken pottery or squares of ceramic tile, you can also make mosaic out of shells, pebbles and even mirror tiles, so you can get all sorts of interesting patterns and textures. One thing I particularly like, though, is making mosaics out of old bottles. You could even make a path out of old beer bottles. Or if you save up your champagne bottles from special occasions, you can turn them upside down and make them into a patch of paving for the patio, so you can relive the memories each time you sit out there. And think of the fun you'll have collecting up the raw materials!

MAKING A BOTTLE MOSAIC

Instead of taking your empties to the bottle bank, save them up and use them to make a bottle mosaic. You don't need a huge area, you can just use the odd square of bottles set in amongst ordinary paving. But if you have enough room and enough empties, you can make a complete path. To achieve a really unusual effect, lay tinfoil underneath your bottles to reflect the light back through them.

1. First, have your party. Dig out the area for the mosaic and level the base. Turn the bottles upside down and space them out so there's a small gap round each one. Blue bottles look prettiest, champagne bottles have big hollows in the bottom, but some brown and green bottles look quite good too. I'd mix up several different kinds.
2. Push any taller bottles down so the bottoms are all level – otherwise you'll have an uneven path.
3. If you are just making a small panel of bottle mosaic, surround the bottles with bricks to keep them firmly in place.
4. Shovel some fine sand all round the bottles – this is the sort sold for children's sand-pits. Leave the top 2 inches of each bottle above the level of the sand, then brush the bits that are left sticking out to clean them.
5. Trickle some ready-mixed sand and cement between the bottles.
6. Push it down well between the bottles so it holds them really firm.
7. A stiffish brush is good for working it into small crevices.
8. Water it well, and leave it to set. The bottle mosaic will be strong enough for you to walk over regularly, so it's fine for a path or an inset in your patio.

DECORATING WITH BOTTLES

If you've made a bottle mosaic, you can carry the theme through and use bottle decorations elsewhere on the patio, with just a very few big structural plants.

* You can make an arrangement of blue bottles turned upside down in a big basket.
* If you have a few champagne bottles that hold special memories for you, you could stand them upright in a special wicker bottle-carrier, which looks quite ornamental standing in a corner – not as if you've just forgotten to clear up after a wild night or anything like that.
* If you do have a party, it's a good idea to stick the empties in a wicker bottle-carrier basket anyway; that way if you don't clear up straight away at least it looks like it's meant to be a decoration.

TILE MOSAICS

Mosaics are a bit like tattoos – tricky to get rid of! There's always the nasty possibility that just as you finish a mega-mosaic it'll suddenly go out of fashion and you'll have to chip it all up and do something else. So tackle a small project first, while you get the hang of it. I'd suggest covering a plant container with mosaic. These are really trendy now. An easy way to start is to buy some mosaic tiles from a DIY store – these are like lots of tiny square tiles stuck to a gauze backing. Buy two different colours. Cut them into strips with scissors. Cover the outside of a clean, dry pot with tile adhesive, and stick strips of tiles round the pot. Start with the lighter colour, then stick a row of darker tiles round near the top to make a Roman-style frieze.

PEBBLE MOSAICS FOR FLOORS

Pebble mosaics are a bit like cobbled pavements to walk over – very knobbly – so I wouldn't make one in the sort of place where you walk all the time. A better idea might be to lift a few paving slabs out of your patio and make small panels of pebble mosaic there instead.

* The easiest method is to put down a dry bed of sand and cement, compact it, then push the pebbles half-way in. You have to sort through your pebbles to pick out those that are the same shape and size, then set them on edge so they make more of a texture.
* Screed over them with more dry sand and cement mix – then water it in. A small pebble mosaic looks good if you just fill it with rows of identical pebbles, but you can also make some lovely features using a light background with dark pebbles picking out a pattern. Or press a ring of oyster-shells in to make a flower shape.

PLANT FILE

I've pulled together here all the best bits about my favourite 'fun' plants with a few extra facts. I won't bore you senseless by telling you all about how to grow them, because my kind of plants are no trouble if you plant them properly and keep them watered. In any case you'll find all the technical stuff on the label that comes with every new plant when you buy it. That sort of information is important, especially when it includes pruning information, so hang on to the label and build up your own garden information 'library'. And if you want to keep your plants tagged, write the name in soft pencil on an aluminium label and push it in alongside the crown or tie it to the branch of a tree – this lasts much longer than a plastic label.

Most plants, unless otherwise stated, grow in normal garden soil – which means any reasonably good ground that has been improved ready for planting. To get the ground ready, take the weeds out and dig in some 'roughage'. You can use well-rotted garden compost, old manure, mushroom compost or second-hand potting compost tipped out of tubs when you take your bedding plants out. If you can't get anything else, buy bags of tree-planting compost or composted bark from a garden centre. If you are planting in spring or summer, sprinkle on some Growmore or blood, fish and bone fertilizer first so it gets dug in too, but don't bother in autumn or winter as it will only get washed away before plants can use it. A complete waste of time and money!

GRASSES AND THINGS THAT AREN'T GRASSES BUT LOOK LIKE THEY OUGHT TO BE

Grassy plants must be among my top favourite plants – I love all of them. Grasses can be big like the giant miscanthus, which looks like ornamental sugarcane and grows 6 feet tall (there are also more decorative smaller ones), or tiny like the tufts of blue festuca grass that are only about 4 to 6 inches high. Some grasses are grown mainly for their foliage, like the yellow Bowles' golden grass, and some for their seed-heads, like the spectacular pennisetums that look like fat hairy caterpillars on stalks. One of my real favourites is the striped *Miscanthus sinensis* 'Zebrinus', because the stripes run the wrong way – lots of plants have vertical stripes, but this one has horizontal rings running round it.

Besides the true grasses you can also get sedges which have grassy-looking leaves – the variegated ones can look brilliant, as some varieties grow into tufts of overlapping fan shapes. Don't assume that all sedges like boggy conditions, because some of them are quite good for pots of drier soil. There are also some slightly unusual perennial plants that have grassy-looking foliage. There's a little one called *Ophiopogon planiscapus* 'Nigrescens' which only grows about 4 inches high but has deep purple-black grassy leaves, and *Liriope muscari* which flowers in autumn – the flower stems look like blue beads stuck on sticks. The thing they all have in common is their leaf shape. Long linear leaves are a really striking shape that goes well with rounded plants like trimmed box 'balls', and specially well with pebbles, which is why they are so good for contemporary gardens.

GREAT BIG CLIMBERS

Giant climbers are good when you want to cover something up in a hurry, like a horrible fence or shed, or you want to make a really wild-looking pergola. You can also let them loose over big shapes made of timber or concrete-reinforcing rods to make a fast-growing plant sculpture or upholstered arch. *Actinidia kolomikta* has quite big leaves that on older plants have violent pink and white tips, which look stunning, as if you have splashed the whole plant with paint. Campsis, pictured, has huge orange-red trumpet flowers which are very South of France for a sunny spot, but it needs a southern garden to flower reliably. And a decorative vine called *Vitis coignetiae* is good for grow-it-yourself dinner plates, as its leaves are really huge and textured, and in autumn they turn outrageous colours.

But my really favourite creative climbers are golden hop and grape-vine, because you can hack both of them back regularly (do it in early spring) and then use the long straggly dried stems for weaving with. You can also train the live stems through trellis or upright poles as they grow, to get a sort of living basketweave effect. With vines, it's worth saving any bits you don't use to burn on the barbecue – cut the stems into short lengths to store, and put two or three at a time on the hot coals when you are cooking for a real holiday atmosphere.

CHOPPABLE PLANTS

If you want trees and shrubs to grow into really interesting gnarled shapes, you can't always rely on them to do it by themselves. To get 'character' plants fast you need to grow the sort you can hack into shape. I love *Cornus controversa* 'Variegata', pictured, which is a shrub that needs a sheltered spot – it does well in a gap in woodland – but its main feature is that its branches grow in tiers like a wedding cake. There's a famous garden in the West Country where they have cut off the lower branches to leave just the top tier, turning it into a wonderful looking flat-topped green and white variegated small tree. Since it doesn't cast a lot of shade, you can plant perennials underneath it right up to the trunk.

Ornamental elders soon make really craggy trees with corky bark if you let them grow, but they are very hackable   just take out odd branches to force the tree into the shape you want. You can also chop them off about 2 feet above the ground every year or two, in spring, to keep them small and bushy, and this makes them grow much bigger leaves than usual – great if you have one of the prettier kinds. You can get different varieties with gold lacy leaves, all-gold leaves, white or yellow variegated leaves and deep plum-purple leaves.

If you really want giant leaves, though, try this. There are several plants that if you left them alone would grow into really enormous trees. So what you do is hack them off just above ground level – literally inches above the soil – every year or two in spring, and they'll then grow incredibly strong straight shoots with massive leaves. The ones to go for are *Paulownia tomentosa*, *Catalpa bignonioides* and *Ailanthus altissima*, but you can also do it with eucalyptus – they all need to have been growing for a few years so they are really well established before you start coppicing them like this – don't do it to a very young one or to other types of tree.

STICK PLANTS

If you want to grow your own sticks for plant supports or withies for basket-weaving, you need certain types of shrubs that will give you the right sort of stems. Grow hazel if you want large quantities of stick-coloured straight stems. Cut well-established hazels back close to the ground every spring to get regular crops of slim stems for making plant supports or weaving hurdles; if you only do it every 3 to 5 years you get thicker stems that make more substantial trellis, uprights for hurdles or even – if you leave them a bit longer – rustic posts.

If you want slim coloured stems for making baskets, plant-support frames and so on, use dogwood (*Cornus alba* 'Westonbirt') or a willow like *Salix alba* 'Chermesina' – both have red stems. Real enthusiasts may like to get a catalogue from a willow specialist who stocks dozens of varieties in all kinds of colours. Cut all the stems off close to the ground in February to 'harvest' them – this also makes the plant grow lots more, which is good as it's only the young stems that have the bright coloured bark. You can also cut some fresh willow stems in summer to stick round the side of a pot to make a 'cage' for bedding plants – the stems take root in the pot, so leave a spray of leaves at the top of each stem as they make a natural flourish for the top.

For curly stems that make good plant supports or natural-looking decorations, stuck in pots of sand on the patio, grow the contorted hazel (*Corylus avellana* 'Contorta') – or if you have really loads of room try the curly willow, *Salix matsudana* 'Tortuosa', though it does get huge. And if you just want tall straight canes to cut, grow bamboo – some varieties have very thin canes and others have thicker ones, which are the strongest if you want to use them the same way as the bamboo canes you buy. You need to let the canes grow for several years before they are ready to cut. Miscanthus, pictured, also has bamboo-like stems which look good but are not very strong – so use them only for lightweight jobs and don't expect them to last more than one season. The old stems die off and dry out naturally after they are a couple of years old, if you don't cut the plant back to tidy it up – then you can just lift them out of the clump.

WATERY PLANTS

The following are all marginal plants that grow with 0 to 4 inches of water over the top of their roots; if you grow them in a pond stand them on a planting shelf so there is up to 4 inches of water over the top of the basket they are growing in. Marginal plants are also good to plant in containers or to keep in pots and stand in a tray with an inch or two of water as a potted bog garden. When you buy new watery plants you could use them in pots in a patio feature first, and move them out to a bog garden or pond later, when they get too big. In autumn, they all need hacking back to about an inch above ground level, or, if they are in a pond, to the top of their planting baskets.

Arum lily (*Zantedeschia aethiopica*) has big greeny-white hood-shaped flowers and huge leaves. Zebra rush (*Schoenoplectus lacustris tabernaemontani* 'Zebrinus' – don't blame me, I didn't make it up!) has rings of white round dark green quill-type leaves – if they turn all-green, it means the plant needs dividing. Corkscrew rush (*Juncus effusus* 'Spiralis') has tightly spiralling leaves which go brown in winter unless you live really far south, so hack it back anyway. Variegated water iris (*Iris laevigata* 'Variegata') is better value than the flowering sort, because although it has flowers too, like most irises they don't last very long, so you are really glad of the green and white striped leaves which look good for the rest of the summer. Water horsetail (*Equisetum hyemale*) has bolt-upright stems like green bamboo with black rings round them. If you want a really stunning contemporary-looking plant to grow in a shiny florist's bucket, this is it.

Gunnera, pictured, is a great plant, as it is so structural. It looks like rhubarb on steroids. The leaves are enormous – the whole plant is. Just stand underneath it and look at the patterns made by the ribs when the sun is shining through the leaves – fantastic. Although you usually see it growing next to water, gunnera looks stunning in a pot but it needs a big one – even so, growing it in a container dwarfs it, so this is the way to keep it smaller if you don't have much room. In winter gunnera dies down but the crown is easily killed off by hard frost, especially when the plant is only young. If you grow it in a pot, move it under cover. Outside, cover the crown with 6 inches of bark chippings for insulation, and then rearrange its own dead leaves over the top to make a tent, with the peak in the middle so it acts like an umbrella and sheds water away from the fat buds. Leave it like that till as late as you can in spring before uncovering it. A late frost will kill off all the early shoots, but it should grow back.

CLIPPABLE PLANTS

Some plants are specially good for clipping tightly into topiary shapes, but always use evergreens so the shape looks good all year round. The classic small topiary plant is box, which is good for growing in pots. The good thing about box is that it's slow-growing and needs clipping only twice a year to keep it tidy. If you want topiary to grow fast, use *Lonicera nitida*, but you'll have to clip it about every 6 weeks to stop it going fuzzy round the edges. If you want a fancy-shaped topiary you need to grow it through a wire-netting frame to help it hold its shape – this also acts as a guide to clip to. Use strong wire to support heads and tails if you want to make something like a peacock. If you just want a dome-shaped topiary with a wide base you don't need a frame, as the plant can support itself. Instead of a normal topiary plant you could grow a nice variegated euonymus, pictured, or a bushy form of rosemary – they all take to being clipped and only need doing once or twice a year.

SPIKY PLANTS

Next to grasses, spiky-shaped plants are essential for a contemporary garden and they go really well with cobbles. They make brilliant feature plants. Hardy outdoor yuccas, like *Yucca gloriosa*, and cordyline palms (*Cordyline australis*) are good, as they naturally grow into very symmetrical shapes. If you have an indoor yucca that's got too big, you could try it outside – they are a lot hardier than people think. I'd plant it out in early summer so it can get going before the first winter, and give it a sheltered spot with very well-drained soil. I can't guarantee it will survive, but it's worth the risk, especially if the alternative is binning it because it's outgrown the living-room.

Phormiums, pictured on page 218, are brilliant, not so spiky but still very structural. The good thing about phormiums is that they come in such amazing colours – as well as the standard green and white striped you can get pink, mauve-purple, peach and almost orange stripes and streaks in the foliage.

AVOID AT ALL COSTS

Okay, this is just a bit of personal self-indulgence I know. You might be crazy about the plants I hate. But it is the end of the book, so here goes anyway.

I'm not mad about anything with speckly variegations – I think they just look sick. In fact, I've seen better-looking plants at death's door. I don't care much for the ordinary *Choisya ternata*, which smells of cat wee, but its golden variety 'Sundance' is simply horrid. I like the green and gold variegated cordylines but the purple ones look like they've got something terminal. Rosemary is great as long as I don't have to eat any more of it. Thanks to my experience at the vineyard, it's even put me off lamb. And personally anything that's not bone-hardy has got to be really special for me to bother with it as I have to share my bedroom with it for the winter, since I don't have a greenhouse. Tree ferns are the exception – I'll always find room for them.

The main thing to avoid, though, is taking gardening too seriously. It's supposed to be what you do to relax. When you catch yourself talking Latin in your sleep or feel a twinge of rake-rage in the herbaceous border, it's time to lighten up. So take my tip: sit in the garden just watching the bees or listening to running water, with a glass of something chilled in your hand. Like they say in New Zealand as they lift the glass, 'Cheers big ears, up your nose curly toes.' It works wonders.

PHOTOGRAPHIC ACKNOWLEDGEMENTS

The photography for *Enjoy Your Garden* was by David Eustace, Roderick Field and Georgia Glynn-Smith.

Additional photographs were kindly supplied by the following photographers:

Christi Carter: 26; Christopher Fairweather: 7; Garden Picture Library/Mark Bolton: 119, 142; John Glover: 13; Harpur Picture Library/Jerry Harpur: 197, 226; Neil Holmes: 222; Michelle Lamontagne: 44, 192; Mayer, le Scanff: 34, 62; Howard Rice: 107, 224; J. S. Sira: 25, 170, 230; Ron Sutherland: 19, 82.

INDEX